ISBN 978-0-9789918-4-5

Published by Convent of the Sacred Heart
1 East 91st Street
New York, NY 10128
www.cshnyc.org

Convent of the Sacred Heart: A History in New York City has been published to commemorate the 125th anniversary of the school.

Project Manager: Craig MacPherson

Writer: Timothy T. Noonan, Heritage Histories

Editors: Craig MacPherson
Christine C. Gowen

Designer: The Blank Page Inc., New York, NY

CONVENT OF THE SACRED HEART:

A History in New York City

This history was made possible by the generosity of
THE PICA AND PECK FAMILIES
in honor of NATALIE PICA '02, MARIEL PICA '11, and ELIZABETH PECK '16.

NEW YORK 2007

"Perfect love has touched us;
the heartbeat of our community is Love;

our hopes for our community are so amazingly high because we have that Love. Our individuality is irreplaceable; but together, we reflect the Love of God, the foundation of 91st Street, lifting Love to unexpected heights. In this we make the good life better; the better, best."

—*MARY RANNEY, RSCJ*

FOREWORD

GOD'S UNSEEN HAND

When I was asked to write the foreword to the history of the Convent of the Sacred Heart at 91st Street, I accepted—and immediately found my internal muse "speechless." How does one present a foreword to 125 years of profound history?

In pondering this task, I started thinking about what was going on around Sacred Heart over the past 125 years. Presidents (24, counting Grover Cleveland twice), mayors (27) and wars (eight, counting undeclared) have come and gone, but the Convent of the Sacred Heart has endured.

But what has gone on around Sacred Heart is not what these past 125 years have been about. It is what has gone on within Sacred Heart that has been the measure that mattered.

What brought you to 91st Street? Was it God's unseen breath that filled your sails one bright morning and sent you and your daughter into the halls of Sacred Heart for that first interview? Or was it just, "If she can get in here, I know she'll get into a great college"? While that may be true, if that is all you hope your daughter gets from a Sacred Heart education, you are paying a full tuition for half an education. For what has been going on within the Convent of the Sacred Heart at 91st Street has been a full education—of mind, body and soul. And not just the soul of the altruist or ethicist but the soul of someone in touch with God.

Janet Erskine Stuart, RSCJ, wrote a hymn many years ago called "Spirit Seeking." One of its poetic expressions might serve well as the foreword to the history and the prologue to the next 125 years—"grasp His unseen hand."

When your daughter graduates from this school, and her foot hits the sidewalk for the first time as an alumna, she joins the ranks of those who walk this Earth, changing it one iota, one gram, one scintilla at a time, grasping God's unseen hand as she does.

Vincent T. Pica II
Father of Natalie '02 and Mariel '11
Board Chairman, 2001–2004

This history is dedicated to

the Religious of the Sacred Heart of Jesus and to the faculty and staff, past and present, who have made our community a beacon of faith, intellect, and compassion in New York City for 125 years.

ACKNOWLEDGEMENTS

Like education in the Sacred Heart tradition, this book would not have been possible without the contributions of time, talent and love of many members of our community.

Much of the path to this book's completion was carved by Christine Unkovic Valentine, Eden Hall '58, whose work on the first history of the school, *Convent of the Sacred Heart, New York City: 1881–1981*, was invaluable in establishing the facts and events of the school's history. It is a wonderful, comprehensive, and insightful history not only of the school, but the spirit behind it. As she exhausted most of the existing materials, large portions of her work were adapted for this book. Simply put, hers is the definitive work and cannot be improved upon. We are deeply indebted to Mrs. Valentine for her tremendous work and generosity in sharing her research and writing.

We are also grateful to Angela Bayo, RSCJ, in New York and Fran Gimber, RSCJ, in St. Louis. Sisters Gimber and Bayo essentially built the archives in New York and provided much insight on the history of Sacred Heart in the United States and in New York City, in particular.

In addition, we offer a very special thank you to all the Religious of the Sacred Heart, alumnae, faculty, parents and trustees who graciously agreed to be interviewed and who shared valuable information for this volume: Jane Reynolds Andrews, Mary Blake, Cathy Curry, Eleanor Fox, RSCJ, Judy Garson, RSCJ, Anna Goddu, Joan Kirby, RSCJ, Jane Maggin, Caroline Samsen Mueller, Rita Gardner Murray, Jane O'Connell, Mimi O'Hagan, Maureen Meehan O'Leary, Barbara Root. We would also like to thank the many people who were not interviewed but whom we have quoted throughout this book, their words taken from various publications in the school archives.

For their expertise in matters grammatical, we thank Eleanor Fox, RSCJ, David Weller, and Michael Aneiro. For all their dedicated efforts in making this book a reality, heartfelt thanks go to: Carolyn Aneiro, Susan Burke, Jennifer Crumlish, Amanda Glatzel, Brooke Gadasi, Paula Howell, Patricia Hult, Marti Ibrahim, Lawson Inman, Vin Pica, Cornelia Thornburgh. For her extraordinary efforts, we also thank Christine Hwong.

For making this book possible with financial assistance, we are indebted to Vincent and JoMarie Pica, and Stephen L. Green and Nancy A. Peck.

the Sacred Heart

TABLE OF CONTENTS

PROLOGUE

Founders and Early Leaders

1779–1841

On the evening of December 12, 1779, ten years before the French Revolution began in Paris with an assault on the Bastille, and 125 kilometers to the southeast in the medieval walled city of Joigny in Burgundy, a fire of unknown origin broke out and raged through the streets. Before the flames were extinguished that night, they spawned a second, spiritual fire that reached around the world and still burns brightly more than two hundred years later.

Statue of St. Madeleine Sophie Barat

MOTHER MADELEINE SOPHIE BARAT

As the fire spread through Joigny that crisp winter evening, Madeleine Fouffé Barat gripped husband Jacques's hands as labor pains overcame her. With Madeleine so close to giving birth, the Barat family could not flee like their neighbors, so they simply prayed the inferno that was swallowing the town would spare their home and their lives. Miraculously, as the conflagration was closing in on the Barat house from both ends of their street, Rue de Puits Chardon, the fire stopped, leaving the houses in the middle—including the Barat's home—untouched.

At 11:00 p.m. the roar of the flames was displaced by the cries of a newborn baby. The child, a little girl, was extremely tiny and dangerously fragile, and so she was christened Madeleine Sophie at five o'clock the next morning with her older brother and a local woman on her way to Mass standing in as godparents.

A woman of the Enlightenment, Madeleine Fouffé Barat passed on her love of books and learning to all her children, and hence her youngest, Madeleine Sophie, grew up in a progressive household devoted to learning. When she was old enough, Madeleine Sophie's big brother and godfather, Louis, brought her to the local college and exposed her to the great writers, such as Ovid, Virgil, and Cervantes. Despite neighbors who mocked the idea of educating a young girl, the Barats persisted, and Madeleine Sophie eventually followed her brother to Paris, where she engaged in even more rigorous academic training.

In Paris she was also exposed to the religious life, but because of the French Revolution, many orders had been disbanded or forced underground. Exhausted from her studies and unable to enter the religious life, Madeleine Sophie returned home briefly during the 1790s. As she matured, secular life held no appeal for her, so she returned to Paris to try to enter an order of Carmelites that, ten years after the Revolution, was struggling to re-establish itself.

While waiting to join the Carmelites, she met a priest by the name of Joseph Varin, a friend of her brother, who was by then a priest. Father Varin was the superior of an association of priests dedicated to the restoration in France of the Society of Jesus. He dreamed of a similar organization that would follow the Jesuit rule and dedicate itself as a cloistered Society committed to the education of young women.

In 1800 Father Varin persuaded Madeleine Sophie to found a religious congregation, which was later called the Religieuses du Sacré-Coeur de Jésus (Religious of the Sacred Heart of Jesus), dedicated to the education of girls. A year later she was named, over her protestations, superior of the society and opened its first school in Amiens, France, just down the Somme from the Channel. Her career as an educator of young women stretched out before her.

MOTHER PHILIPPINE DUCHESNE

About 350 miles to the southeast of Amiens, in Grenoble, France, another young woman from a prominent family, Philippine Duchesne, was following a similar path to that of Mother Barat. Liberally educated like Madeleine Sophie, Philippine was also drawn to the religious life and had developed a particular call to minister to a

Portrait of Philippine Duchesne

Illustration of Madeleine Sophie with Philippine Duchesne pleading to be sent to North America

population she had never met: Native Americans, about whom she had learned from missionaries who visited her family's home.

Also like Madeleine Sophie Barat, Philippine Duchesne saw her plans to enter a religious congregation undermined by the French Revolution. In 1801, about the time Mother Barat was named superior of the Sacred Heart school in Amiens, Philippine was joining with other women in Grenoble to restore a convent and school that had been closed by the Revolution.

By late 1804, the school in Grenoble had come to the attention of Mother Barat, who traveled from Amiens to see it and to meet Philippine. By the next spring Philippine had joined Madeleine Sophie's congregation.

TO AMERICA

Mother Barat, now superior general of the Society of the Sacred Heart, brought Mother Duchesne up from Grenoble to serve as secretary general at the Society's headquarters in Paris. However, when Monsignor William DuBourg, the Bishop of Louisiana in America, arrived on a visit with a special request for Mother Barat to send some nuns to his far-flung outpost, Mother Barat entrusted Mother Duchesne with the assignment. Mother Duchesne left almost immediately for America, with four other nuns.

The vision Mother Duchesne carried forth, to educate women both in mind and in spirit, was unique, born of Mother Barat's perspective on the importance of women in Christ's overall plan of redemption. "How rare it is to find a valiant woman!" Mother Barat had written.

It is perhaps necessarily so, since Scripture says that they are more precious than pearls and diamonds. Let us however work to train a few. For in this century we must no longer count on men to preserve the faith. The grain of faith that will be saved will hide itself among women.

A woman cannot remain neutral in the world. She too is sent for the fall and resurrection of many. How different are God's thoughts from ours! Between women and God is often arranged the eternal salvation of husbands and sons. But for this she must be valiant. Strong to uphold purity of life. Strong to keep inviolate the treasure of faith. Strong in every battle of life. Great-souled in the face of calamity, persecution and death. And remember, sorrow is the training ground of strong souls.

After months at sea and suffering from scurvy like many seafarers, Mother Duchesne and her small band of religious landed in New Orleans in 1818. After a brief rest, they embarked on another 40-day trip up the Mississippi to an assignment 20 miles west of St. Louis in St. Charles, Missouri, just on the other side of the Missouri River.

In St. Charles, a tiny cluster of hovels and lean-tos, Mother Duchesne established the first Sacred Heart school in America. So spartan were the accommodations in the single-room building that each morning the nuns moved their beds out of the way to make room for their ten students. Mother Duchesne struggled with English, which she never fully mastered, and many of the children were destitute. She implemented the Society's Plan of

France

Key locations that signify the beginning of Madeleine Sophie Barat's goals to educate young women

Portrait of Mother Aloysia Hardey

Studies and Code of Discipline, which incorporated the spiritual and academic ideals outlined by Mother Barat, as well as she could under difficult circumstances.[1]

Over the next several years, she opened, then closed, a boarding school in St. Charles and a third school in Florissant, 20 miles away. Mother Duchesne briefly traveled back to Louisiana before returning to Missouri to found an American base, or mother house, for the Society of the Sacred Heart in St. Louis. The "City House," as it was called, included a convent school, a free school, a chapel, and an orphanage.

MOTHER ALOYSIA HARDEY

In New York City, Bishop John Dubois heard of the Society's work and requested that Mother Barat send some nuns to open a school in his diocese. "There is no doubt as to the success of an order like yours in this city," he wrote. "Indeed it is greatly needed.... I believe one of your schools, commenced with sufficient money to purchase property and support itself until the ladies have time to make themselves known, would succeed beyond all our expectations."

Mother Aloysia Hardey, a former student of Mother Duchesne and the superior of a school in St. Michael's, Louisiana, was sent to New York to meet the Bishop's request. With three other nuns, Elizabeth Galitzin, Catherine Thiefry, and Johanna Shannon, she moved

1 In 1805, members of the Society drew up the first of eleven formulations of a Plan of Studies to provide a guide for teachers in their mission to educate "the whole woman with a view to her own vocation in the circumstances and the age in which she has to live" (1952 formulation). Over the next 150 years, Sacred Heart schools adhered to a single unified curriculum.

Our Network

The Network of Sacred Heart Schools, an association dedicated to the values of Christian education articulated by Madeleine Sophie Barat, provides a means for mutual support and development among the schools through sharing of intellectual, spiritual, and other resources in furthering the mission of Sacred Heart education. Today there are 21 schools in the Network, along with two affiliate schools and one provisional school.

ACADEMY OF THE SACRED HEART

St. Charles, Missouri

The Academy in St. Charles was the first Sacred Heart school in America. When St. Philippine Duchesne came to the New World in 1818, Bishop DuBourg had rented for her a large log cabin, locally known as the Duquette Mansion (named for its size, not its refinement!), which became the first free school west of the Mississippi. Difficult living conditions and the lack of boarding students prompted a move to nearby Florissant after just one year. However, in 1828 the Religious returned to the Duquette Mansion, and in 1835, the Society erected the first brick convent and school. That historic building remains to this day and is the central core of the school's ten-acre campus. The Academy continued to operate as a private school for girls until 1972, when it began admitting boys into the early grades. Today, the Academy is the largest independent elementary school in the metropolitan St. Louis area, with 650 children in pre-primary through eighth grade. An accelerated academic program, extensive community service, and lifelong connections with students and their families are hallmark features of the Academy in St. Charles. The school is justifiably proud of its heritage as the cradle of Sacred Heart education in America and cherishes the words of St. Madeleine Sophie Barat in a letter to Philippine: "I hold firmly to St. Charles, and I am delighted that we have a house there. It may accomplish more good than any other house."

into a boarding house at 412 Houston Street and opened the first Sacred Heart school in the East in 1841.

Mother Hardey remained as superior until 1844, when she was named Mother Superior for Eastern North America. She went on to help found nearly 30 convents in the eastern U.S., Canada, and Cuba.

A MISSION FULFILLED

In late 1852, 34 years after she arrived in the U.S. and ten years after the school on Houston Street had been founded, Mother Duchesne passed away in St. Charles, Missouri. Late in her life the Bishop of St. Louis had recalled her from a brief posting with the Potowatomi Indians on the frontier because of her advanced age. Against her will and amid a sense of failure, she had dutifully returned to the convent she had founded in St. Charles, heartbroken that she had spent only one unfulfilling year of her life with the Native Americans among whom she had wanted to live and teach since childhood.

Mother Duchesne could perhaps have assuaged her own sense of failure by remembering Mother Sophie's words: "For the sake of a single child I would have founded the Society." Clearly, Mother Duchesne had already met that criterion hundreds of times over as a result of her work. At her death in 1852, the Society of the Sacred Heart was fully established in the United States with the City House in St. Louis and two dozen schools throughout North America, from Louisiana to Nova Scotia.

First New York convent, Houston and Mulberry Streets, later Convent of Sisters of Mercy

"I found my Sacred Heart education both spiritually enriching and inspirational, because I didn't feel like people were putting up walls around us. We were allowed to be open, to think, speak, and express ourselves freely."

—ELLEN McCURLEY '77

GOOD
VERY GOOD
INDIFFERENT
TRES BIEN

CHAPTER 1

Building a Firm Foundation

1841–1914

Between 1840 and 1880, America was becoming a different, more industrial world. The age of the machine was ushering in great empires, such as John D. Rockefeller's Standard Oil and Andrew Carnegie's steel mills. Great factories were blossoming like brick jungles, and the railroads were their steel roots, reaching deep into the soil of American commerce from the Atlantic to the Pacific.

Congested traffic on 53rd Street heading toward Fifth Avenue

The growth of business led to the growth of cities, as millions flocked to the great urban areas for factory or retail jobs. America was becoming an urban nation, and New York, which in 1880 had grown to six times its 1840 size, had become its crown jewel.

A succession of Sacred Heart schools struggled to serve this growing metropolis. A few years after it had opened on Houston Street, the nuns moved the boarding portion of the school to the Delafield House, Ravenswood, in Astoria, leaving the academy, or day school, in place back on Houston.[2]

Soon after the boarding school moved, a free school for forty children was opened at Houston Street, in line with Mother Barat's directive and tradition of running a free school wherever there was a Sacred Heart academy. In 1845, both the day and free schools left Houston Street to set up in rented quarters on Bleecker Street.

The schools remained at Bleecker Street for only two years before closing. After a brief period, during which there was no Sacred Heart day school in Manhattan at all, a second house was rented on Bleecker Street, and an academy with an enrollment of 60 girls between the ages of six and thirteen was established there in February 1848.

In 1851 the religious moved their community to another building on West 14th Street, where they had been asked to open a school for the children of immigrants. Additionally, the nuns hosted a night school for working women, the academy with 80 students,

2 A convent was technically the cloister where the religious lived; an academy or convent school was a private school; a free school was a school for the poor or underpriveleged, without tuition.

a Sunday school for 150 youngsters, and religious instruction for large numbers of women from the surrounding neighborhoods. To obtain permanent and larger quarters, land was bought and the construction of a four-story building was begun.

In 1855, these various parts of the Sacred Heart community in Manhattan moved into the newly erected building at 49 West 17th Street. In the 1854–1855 Lettres Annuelles, the circular letters that informed the Sacred Heart communities in various countries of one another's activities, this building was described as "well built, well lighted, and well aired ... planned to accommodate large numbers without crowding and to carry on diversified works without confusion."

By 1881, after these various start-ups and relocations, there were two schools in New York: the one that had been on 17th Street in lower Manhattan since 1855, and the other in the old Lorillard estate on St. Nicholas Heights, near Manhattanville, where the school in Astoria had moved in 1847. It was determined that these two schools could no longer accommodate the exploding population of New York. Manhattanville was considered too far north for day students to access, and the school at 17th Street was now well south of the center of town. Thus, a new academy was founded in a brownstone at the corner of Madison Avenue and 54th Street to meet the need for a day school in the city's new prime residential section. The launch of this new school is considered today to be the official beginning of the school that would eventually become the Convent of the Sacred Heart at 91st Street.

In 1855, the 17th Street building housed all of the "diversified works" of the Society in Manhattan.

Juniors' Study Hall at the Madison Avenue school

Reverend Mother Sarah Jones led the small community that opened the new school. "With entire approbation and warm welcome to the Cathedral Parish," and with her assistants, Margaret Hoey and Louise Bouvier, whose family were benefactors of the house, and three or four other religious, she welcomed 36 pupils that first year. On September 29, 1881, eight days after classes began, their new neighbor, His Eminence Cardinal McCloskey, with his secretary, the Reverend John Farley, who would later become Cardinal Archbishop of New York, gave their official blessing to the convent and school by celebrating the first Mass there.

From the beginning, the modest and warmly remembered house seems to have had the atmosphere that Mother Barat had described as ideal for Sacred Heart residences: "A house of the Sacred Heart where reign silence, charity, and regularity is a little paradise .... Everyone in this household is happy and contented; they are more and more attached to their vocation because the Lord always gives one hundredfold for sacrifices that are made with love, fidelity, and generosity."

Partly because there was more space, enrollment more than doubled in the Academy's third year, and two classes were added, necessitating the purchase of an adjoining brownstone to allow enrollment to grow.

The school, with Mother Barat's approval, accepted Protestant children, a bold and visionary step that caused some initial friction and objections. Many years later, however, at the time of Madeleine Sophie Barat's canonization, bishops from many areas wrote to Rome, speaking of the Sacred Heart religious as effective missionaries and supporting Mother Barat's decision

The Madison Avenue school

THE CURRICULUM AT THE *Madison Avenue School*

AN EARLY ANNOUNCEMENT OF THE ACADEMY'S GOALS, CURRICULUM, AND TERMS WAS SUCCINCT:

The aim of the Religious of the Sacred Heart is to give their pupils an education which will prepare them to fill worthily the place for which Divine Providence destines them. The training of character and the cultivation of manners are, therefore, considered matters of primary importance.

Hours of attendance are from 9 a.m. to 3:30 p.m. Classes in the junior department end at three o'clock.

It will not be necessary for the pupils to study lessons, or to write compositions at home, as time will be allotted for this purpose during school hours.

The pupils will dine at one o'clock and will be required to converse in French, while at table.

The course of studies comprises, besides the thorough grounding in the ordinary branches of education:

- A complete course of Christian Doctrine.
- Elements of Christian Philosophy.
- Ancient and Modern History, special attention being given to Sacred and Church History.
- Literature, Ancient and Modern.
- The English Language in all its branches.
- Latin.
- Mathematics, and
- The Natural Sciences.

Terms.

- Senior Department – $200 per annum
- Junior Department – $150 per annum
- Bills payable, semi-annually, in advance.

References required.

TOP: 7th Grade class of the Madison Avenue school, 1925
BOTTOM: Madison Avenue school students in their winter uniforms, 1929

to allow non-Catholics access to the special experience of Sacred Heart education.

TRADITIONS AND THE TRAINING OF CHARACTER

The Madison Avenue school journals kept by the nuns reveal little about the day-to-day life of the school, which must have been taken for granted as a continuation of the traditions that had so quickly sprung up and crystallized since Mother Barat founded her first school in 1801.

Holy days and special visitors are noted in the journals, but the world outside is seldom glimpsed. It must be remembered that until the late 20th century the Religious of the Sacred Heart were semi-cloistered; for the most part, excursions from the Madison Avenue convent had as their destination one of the other New York schools, in which daily life, both in the convent and in the school, followed the same patterns and rhythms.

Madeleine Sophie Barat had often stated that her life's work would be well spent for the betterment of a single child. Her followers lived out this commitment intensely but quietly, uninterested in gaining the attention of the world at large. In 1865, when the foundress died, there were 28 Sacred Heart institutions in the United States. Madison Avenue, which was subsequently added to their number, had no need to invent new academic rituals or courses. It was linked from the outset with a fully developed plan, well summarized in 1913 by the Society's superior general, Janet Erskine Stuart:

Congé

From the French for leave-taking or farewell, congé is a day when students and teachers take leave of their regular studies and channel their energy into having fun. Congés come when they are least expected, since the planning for them is done in secret. Originally, the activities and games, such as cache-cache (a group form of hide-and-seek), were planned by the religious for the girls of the boarding schools. The tradition has carried over to many Sacred Heart schools of today, and congé continues to provide school communities a welcome day of relaxation and merriment.

Ribbons

Another form of recognition in Sacred Heart schools was ribbons. Ribbons, worn diagonally from a student's right shoulder and fastened on the left at the waist to allow the ends to fall free to skirt length, have long been marks of distinction in Sacred Heart schools. Students in the third and fourth years of high school, classes traditionally termed Third and Fourth Academics, wore blue ribbons, while those in the first and second years (First and Second Academics) wore green. Students in the middle school grades also wore green ribbons; lower grade students wore pink ribbons, with red ribbons reserved for first and second grades. The high school ribbons were awarded by a vote of the students, ratified by the Religious, in recognition of good conduct, good spirit, helpful influence, and leadership.

BELOW: Students wearing blue ribbons, 1957

> The Society of the Sacred Heart has its own programme of studies, of which the foundations and principles are the same in all schools of the same grade, and the superstructure is adapted to the wants of each country in which this Society has founded houses .... The object, when it was drawn up, was to enable those who had gone through it to judge wisely of persons and things, to distinguish between "the precious and the vile" in questions of literature, art, taste, conduct, and manners; and the studies which conduced most effectually to this end were considered relatively the most important. Next in order came those that were useful, and afterwards those that were considered at the time merely ornamental.

Probably due to the complaints of the students—or perhaps they were boasting—it was well-known that the Academy on Madison Avenue, like all Sacred Heart schools, was strict. Mother Janet Erskine Stuart gave the Society's definitive answer to those who disapproved of enforced silence between classes, marching in ranks, curtsying to the Reverend Mother, and the like, and at the same time frankly acknowledged the schools' critics:

> The discipline in schools of the Sacred Heart has met with a great deal of criticism. Why these moments of strict silence? Why this supervision? Why this insistence on play? This opposition to sets and cliques and private friendships? Why these exercises in behaviour, like formal parade? Why such exacting persistence as to manners? All, in the main, for the same reason: because they conduce to the training of character; they exact self-control, and attention, and consideration for others, and remembrance, not in one way, but in a hundred ways.

One of the "exercises in behaviour" that was repeated weekly at Sacred Heart schools around the world was known as "prîmes."[3] The exercise is remembered vividly by most who experienced it. White-gloved, the assembled student body waited in silence for the entrance of Reverend Mother. One class at a time, students were called to form a semicircle in front of Reverend Mother and their teachers. Two by two, students would curtsy to the imposing figure and then receive from her hand a small card that testified to the student's conduct of the past week. The few who received cards marked "bien" or "assez bien," instead of the hoped-for "très bien," felt a momentary sting of censure, and they were expected to resolve themselves to better behavior for the coming week. Peer pressure played its role, too; classes in which too many girls were handed "bien" cards—which in this setting translated roughly as "satisfactory"—might have coveted privileges denied them.

At this exercise, which took place every Monday at 11:00 a.m. at Madison Avenue, academic achievement was also honored. Medals were distributed to show which students had excelled in English or history or other subjects. The medals were to be worn for the whole week, but the little cards were returned immediately after prîmes, to be saved by the thrifty nuns for the following week's round.

"The idea in the schools of the Sacred Heart," Mother Stuart explained, no doubt with criticisms of

3 *Prîmes were held on the fist (prime) day of the week, which was Monday for day schools and Sunday for boarding schools.*

The Students

The Register of the Pupils listed each pupil's name, address, and class, and where she continued her education after leaving Madison Avenue. Many transferred to another Sacred Heart academy for the final "graduating class," equivalent to the first year of college and offered only at the Society's boarding schools. Among the early students, a number went on to the two other New York schools, Seventeenth Street and Manhattanville. Some attended Sacred Heart schools elsewhere in the country, from Louisiana to California, and a few traveled to schools in Canada and France. During Madison Avenue's first 25 years, five alumnae entered the religious life. Loretta Reilly, Josephine McGinnis, and Teresa Mooney took the vows of the Religious of the Sacred Heart; Camille Huerstel became a Helper of the Holy Souls and Jessie Lynch became a Holy Child nun.

ABOVE: Senior graduation at the Madison Avenue school, class of 1913

THE *French* SCHOOL

The directive from the mother house was clear: the language of a school's country was to prevail in each house, and indeed, English was the primary language of instruction. Nevertheless, French was ever present, and not only in its instruction as a foreign language. A few lines of the Academy's statement on goals and curriculum were in French, and the terms were repeated on the reverse in French. French was heard often at lunchtime conversations, and terminology for many school functions, such as the use of "congés" for "school holidays," was French. So common was French, in fact, that for some years the Academy was known to New Yorkers as "the French school."

prîmes in mind, "is to allow each child to be itself, and to surround it with an atmosphere of so much attentive affection that it may be unconstrained, and let out the real self with its good as well as its weak points, thus becoming known, so that it may be taken in hand to correct its defects, and taught to know and control itself."

THE TWENTY-FIFTH YEAR

By the turn of the century, the Society was celebrating its centenary, and several generations of New York women had been educated by "the Madames of the Sacred Heart." In 1902, these graduates formed the Madison Avenue school's first alumnae association. By 1905, as the school approached its 25th year, the enrollment had continued to grow to nearly a hundred students, necessitating the purchase of a third house, which was connected to the neighboring houses through interior passages.

Sodality activities, contributing to the needs of New Yorkers, had been attached to the convents from the beginning, and to celebrate the upcoming anniversary, the directress of the Children of Mary at Manhattanville proposed that the alumnae and the sodalists of Madison Avenue, Maplehurst (the new home of the 17th Street academy, at 174th Street and University Avenue), and Manhattanville join forces in one major effort. Their choice involved the education of women: they established, financed, and staffed the Barat Industrial School in a rented house on East Houston Street. One of its goals was to train young

Students from the Madison Avenue School pose for a class picture in 1929. BACK ROW, FROM RIGHT TO LEFT: Helen Mooney, Kakia Liasco, Lucille Berizzi, and Edwina Atwell FRONT: Susan Close, Mary Ellen Goodwin, and Constance Heide

Chapel at the Madison Avenue School

women for jobs in retailing. In 1911, the school was moved to another house in Little Italy, on Chrystie Street, and renamed the Barat Settlement.

Other alumnae activities early in this century add to the picture of intellectually active and socially concerned Sacred Heart graduates. For 20 years, their Bohemian Guild worked with 250 children annually. At the night school in the Madison Avenue house, begun in 1905 and soon enrolling more than a hundred women, alumnae offered courses in religion, business, English, and sewing. And Les Abeilles de Ste Catherine, a group dedicated to literary pursuits, held meetings to discuss philosophy and articles and books on current events.

By its 25th year, 1906, and now in three neighboring brownstones, the Madison Avenue academy had more than a hundred students. Mass was offered on September 29 to commemorate the first Mass said in the chapel a quarter-century before. "Despite their worldly milieu," it was felt that "real progress in more serious work" was being made with the students. "They are unaffected, docile, with sufficient resources of initiative and of generosity, and know how to live their faith."

The convent enjoyed many visitors during these years. The bishop of New Zealand, upon visiting it, exclaimed of the nuns, "They all smile!" Another visitor, Archbishop Farley of New York, attended the students' pageants in December 1906, and asked them if they appreciated the grace of being at Sacred Heart. "For me," he said, "there is no better education, but what

A sunny corner in one of the Junior classrooms, 1929. From left: Anne Murray, Esther Ridder, Josephine Crowley, and Mary Hoy

The "Boardwalk" on the roof of the Madison Avenue building where the religious could enjoy outdoor activity.

responsibilities it imposes!" Cardinal Logue, primate of Ireland, may have been the children's favorite visiting dignitary, for he granted them two holidays, or congés, as they were called in the Sacred Heart schools.

One of the school's most distinguished visitors, and one of the Society's most extraordinary members, arrived for five days at the end of May 1914. Mother Janet Erskine Stuart visited Madison Avenue in her capacity as Superior General during a worldwide tour of all convents and schools under her leadership. Her comments, entered in the "Memorial of Visits" in her firm hand, add to our view of a busy place:

> This house strikes me very favourably by its religious spirit and tone, the union of mind and heart which appears in almost all, and the spirit of earnest study and attachment to the house which distinguish the school.
>
> I learn from outside that the Children of Mary are at the head of all that is best in the good work of New York. But the efforts to keep them up to a worthy standard in dress and social intercourse are only partially successful against the strong tide of worldliness which runs so high in New York. The old pupils are said to go through a great deal and remain unspoiled. It will be a saving and sanctifying element in their lives if they will give and continue to give their personal service to the poor of Christ.
>
> I beg the blessing of God on this devoted and religious Community and pray that the house may be a center of prayer and spiritual strength from which many souls may draw help and comfort.

Five months later, this accomplished educator passed away at age 57, exhausted from her world travels and from the dangers she faced during the first months of World War I. Her message to New York's Convent of the Sacred Heart is one of its treasured possessions.

"The world inside 91st Street remains a timeless one because it lives in the heart of Saint Madeleine Sophie's vision. We come as we are, offering the gifts we have been given, to serve the mission of the Sacred Heart: forming and empowering young women to make the world better."

—SUZANNE PRICE
former Head of Upper School

Sodalities

Dating back to the origins of the Society of the Sacred Heart in post-Revolutionary France, the sodalities were an important dimension of the spiritual education in Sacred Heart schools. In 1832, since the rule of cloister prevented the religious from leaving their convents, Mother Barat organized a group of former students in Lyon to perform works of service, especially for the poor and needy. From these roots grew sodalities, religious organizations that students could elect to join, each dedicated to a particular ideal, as well as the performance of good works and an adherence to the dictates of the Catholic faith. The four sodalities in the 91st Street community were the Aspirants to Children of Mary, the Angels Sodality, the Aspirants to the Angels, and the Aloysian Society. While the aims of these religious fellowships are met in different ways today, in some Sacred Heart schools members of the former sodalities still gather for prayer and reflection.

CHAPTER 2

We Will Someday Live In This House

1914–1934

Even before Mother Stuart's death in 1914, a series of events in Europe began to cast a dark shadow over the world. In June of that year, Franz Ferdinand, Archduke of Austria and heir to the Austro-Hungarian throne, was assassinated in Sarajevo. Within months Germany had aligned behind Austria, and Russia and England behind Serbia. German U-boats began sinking English ships, and in May of 1915, the cruise ship

An early photo of Manhattanville College

Lusitania, with numerous Americans on board, was sunk off the south coast of England. By 1917 American soldiers were headed overseas to take part in "the Great War."

Many private boys' schools lost students, faculty, and particularly alumni to the war. As a girls' school run by nuns, Madison Avenue was spared this unhappy circumstance, and school life proceeded pretty much as normal. But in keeping with Sacred Heart's focus on the needs of the larger world, students contributed to the war effort, according to the journal, by devoting the morning of a congé, in one instance, to making bags for the soldiers.

A few years later, with the war over, the United States entered the high-spirited Jazz Age, an especially exciting time for a young girl in New York, surrounded by the energy of new intellectualism, new music, and a culture in full celebration. While music and celebration abounded, in the more intellectual arenas artists like Man Ray and Pablo Picasso and writers like Gertrude Stein, Ezra Pound, Ernest Hemingway, and F. Scott Fitzgerald were breaking new ground in their respective fields. Educators at Sacred Heart and other institutions who endeavored to stay current were challenged to keep up with the new world around them.

THE SOCIETY REACHES OUT

In this dizzyingly optimistic and mostly bountiful time, the Society of the Sacred Heart leveraged global enthusiasm to extend its reach and service throughout the world. The Mother House, after a brief stay in

Belgium, had moved to Rome, and new schools were opened throughout the 1920s in the United States, Puerto Rico, China, India, and Peru. Sacred Heart education also reached the African continent, where classes were sometimes taught without benefit of a formal school. Some schools had been opened to boys, and secular teachers were increasingly welcomed into the fold.

In the United States, Mother Duchesne's and Mother Hardey's work had continued. The early expansion in the eastern United States, Canada, and Cuba had been matched in the West as the St. Louis and Grand Coteau schools had spawned others in Louisiana, Missouri, Nebraska, Washington, Texas, California, and British Columbia. Though she died feeling a failure because she only spent one year with Native Americans, Mother Duchesne had more than fulfilled her mission of seeding the new world with superior academic opportunities for young women.

In the New York vicariate, the 17th Street school, which had begun at Bleecker Street, had ultimately migrated to Noroton, Connecticut, in 1924, and the Houston Street day school had ended up at Maplehurst. Manhattanville College had been certified as a college by the Regents in 1917, and the Pius X School of Music, housed at Manhattanville, had been founded a year later.

The year 1925, the height of the Roaring Twenties, represented a significant milestone for Madison Avenue and for all Sacred Heart schools throughout the world. Pope Pius XI would canonize society founder Madeleine Sophie Barat, who had, at least in terms of the education

In the Madison Avenue School garden, seventh grade students are dressed for St. Madeleine Sophie's Feast Day, 1925. BACK ROW: Dorothy Mooney, Virginia Hush, Marie Virginia Moore. MIDDLE ROW: Moira Kenedy, Natalie Calmer, Erdwine Poole,Kitty Manners Wagner, Marjorie Culkin, Mary Elizabeth Kenny. FRONT ROW: Matilde Mittendorf, Rosemary Roche Ryan

2
94
13
18

THE FEAST OF *Saint Madeleine Sophie Barat* May 25, 1925

The Feast of Saint Madeleine Sophie occurs every year on May 25th. The journal records the event on the special year of Mother Barat's canonization:

"The children came in white and at 9:30 sang the Solemn High Mass. It was their first attempt and they had practiced for weeks. They left the chapel after Mass and returned in half an hour for the panegyric preached by Rev. Father Fadden. E. de M. [Children of Mary] of last year's Fourth Academic Class came to take charge of the smallest Juniors during that time. Then Fr. Fadden received a number of children into the Congregation of Angels, St. Aloysius and the Holy Child. At dinner each one found at her place a copy of our Mother General's circular letter to the children. At 12:30 all went to their class rooms and at 12:45 each class entertained its Mistress and offered good wishes. At 1:30 all assembled in the Reception Room where a small ivory-tinted statue of Our Mother stood in the centre of the stage, surrounded by red and gold flowers and lights. At her feet was the motto chosen by the school as their own—'Fide fundata' (founded on faith).

"First came the recitation of 'The Making of a Blessed Saint,' then the Roehampton hymn and then a short address. Reverend Mother then gave each one a medal and spoke to them of our Saint and their motto. The Juniors were dismissed and the Seniors sang during Solemn Benediction, followed by the veneration of the relic."

No one knew a second holiday celebrating the canonization would follow the very next day.

of women, used enlightened thinking to challenge religious and social dogma a century earlier.

On May 25th of that year the school celebrated the annual feast of Blessed Madeleine Sophie Barat by suspending classes in favor of games, songs, prayers, and pageants. Through this feast day, plans for a subsequent canonization holiday had been kept a profound secret. On the day after the feast, May 26, the school enthusiastically received the proclamation made by a Papal herald of the gift of a holiday. The students, of course, were joyous, having arrived at school that morning and greeted their teachers in full anticipation of a day of classes.

The holiday began immediately after the announcement, with everyone proceeding to the Chapel, where the picture of Saint Madeleine Sophie was still enthroned above the altar, surrounded by lilies and roses, and making the offering of the day in her honor. A variety of celebrations culminated in an impromptu dialogue and pageant in the Reception Room, ending with a tableau of Saint Madeleine Sophie in glory.

THE SCHOOL ON MADISON AVENUE

On May 27, 1926, a year after Mother Barat's canonization, the Regents of the University of the State of New York granted the school at Madison Avenue state recognition, or accreditation. Inside their three brownstones on 54th Street, amidst all the activity from the outside world and outreach from the Society, the Religious of the Sacred Heart of Jesus of "The Female Academy of the Sacred Heart," as it was formally titled by the Regents, glided silently about the halls in their black robes

TOP: The reception room at the Madison Avenue school
BOTTOM: The Senior study hall at the Madison Avenue school

keeping a wary eye on their 130-plus charges, all in uniform, who passed between classes in respectful silence. Tuition had nearly doubled since 1881, but the basic plan of studies, as printed in the school's brochures, was almost identical, including the notification "References Required." The young ladies mostly adhered to the rules, but they were always conscious of the rollicking world swirling about them, as if they represented the calm eye of an especially violent cultural storm. And the religious maintained their iron grip and tight rules, as outlined by Mother Barat over a century before.

Students from the era well remember the discipline, both inside the classroom and out. Mother Simpson, for instance, a large woman who taught fifth grade and made students repeat any homework that was not up to snuff, made an impression on students, but not as much of one as the ancient and stern Mother McCarthy. "Mother McCarthy presided over a small group of little girls," said Isabelle Stricker Kelly '38. "She used a brass-tipped pointer to point out 'bat, cat, fat, hat,' etc., from a flip chart. It was a tiny room, a sewing room, I think, and we sat on little chairs."

Isabelle Kelly went on to note that Mother McCarthy was certainly the school's last direct connection with the Society's founder. "Mère McCarthy had gone to Paris as a young girl and had made her vows before St. Madeleine Sophie Barat in the mid 19th century."

It is safe to say that there were no Jazz Age flappers at Madison Avenue in the 1920s, but despite the nuns' best efforts, the world still found its way, through the high spirits of the girls, inside the walls of Sacred Heart.

Academically all the discipline helped support the same rigor of 50 years before, but the Plan of Studies for all Sacred Heart schools had evolved over the previous century. By the 1920s, according to a note in the archives, the "French curriculum of studies has been modified to suit the needs of another age, and now the Academic Classes are fitted to meet the requirements of the College when the students leave here." (The College, of course, was Manhattanville, where so many graduates were simply expected to go.) Christian doctrine and the Elements of Christian Psychology still anchored the curriculum, but students engaged in a broad study of the liberal arts regularly found themselves reading such classics as Shakespeare and Dickens. Classes were held between 9:00 a.m. and 2:15 p.m. for the junior school, where tuition was $350, and 9:00 a.m. and 2:45 p.m. for the senior school, where tuition was $400. Students wore green cloth dresses, green coats, tan blouses, tan gloves, and tan stockings, all of which had to be purchased in addition to tuition. Sports—mostly field hockey and basketball—were held nearby.

The Madison Avenue school community also continued to run numerous activities outside the school during this era. The Children of Mary sodality, dedicated to serving New York's poor, numbered 300 members from the surrounding area. Many alumnae made clothes at home or came on special sewing evenings to support the group and also to make altar linens for poor churches. The Mater Admirablis Club instructed young businesswomen in spiritual matters, and the Barat Settlement, where pupils sometimes went to entertain as many as 50 or 60 kindergarteners, was managed

Seniors at the Madison Avenue school, 1934
FRONT ROW: Zita Devlin, Jean Mulcahy, Regina Weston.
BACK ROW: Joanna Miller, Marie Bolger, Dorothy Heide, Joan Bassler, Marie Murray

"...a day in the country"

Children from the Barat Settlement visit Madison Avenue for "a day in the country," 1932

with the two other local Sacred Heart schools. Mission benefits were also held from time to time, such as the one at the Plaza for the newly founded Sacred Heart school in Shanghai, or others to help Mother Daniel, M.D., and Gavin Duffy, S.J, who were working as missionaries in India.

A NEW HOME

In 1926, the same year the school was certified by the Regents of the State of New York, the realty firm of Pease and Elliman was retained to spearhead the search for a new home. In the midst of a half-century of area schools moving from one place to another in New York, Madison Avenue had remained where it had been since its founding in 1881, on the corner of 54th Street.

The three connected four-story brownstones had been suitable for the better part of 50 years as young girls climbed the dozen steps to the front doors and played on the stone handrails as they entered the old residences. The rigors of the years were finally beginning to show, though, and expansion, as had occurred when the second, then the third house had been bought, was no longer possible. The chapel, for example, was beautiful with its white ceiling and exposed beams, but it was narrow and tiny like many brownstone rooms and held only 100, or about 70 percent of the school community. Classrooms were crowded, and amenities were few. Students didn't even have a place to hang their coats and rest their schoolbags or lunches, except on the boards which had been placed over the original free-standing tubs in the bathrooms.

In 1928, as the nuns continued their search for a new home, Herbert Hoover ran for office predicting an end to poverty in America, but unfortunately, on October 29, 1929, less than a year after his election, the bottom fell out of the economy with the stock market crash, and poverty swept over America as it never had before.

The next two Septembers saw further drops in enrollment. In those grim years, the tuition and luncheon fee of $400 annually for the Upper School and $350 for the Lower School, with "Books, Stationery, and Diction extra," must have burdened parents considerably. Then there were the necessities: two green cloth dresses at $19.50, and the requisite tan oxfords could run as high as $5.00. No doubt requests for scholarship aid increased as enrollment declined. From the beginning, the religious helped some parents with partial tuition relief, entered in the accounts as "fractions," and occasionally by accepting a girl gratis.

In 1931, at the depth of the Depression, Madison Avenue approached its Golden Jubilee, the Fiftieth Anniversary of its founding. Few Sacred Heart schools in the East had remained in one location for so long. In celebration, and as if to underscore the fact that relocation had been dropped, the chapel was renovated "with befitting solemnity, joy and thanksgiving" by one of the Children of Mary for the occasion.

Sometime during that Golden Jubilee year, as breadlines still wound through New York's streets and makeshift shantytowns still clustered in the shadows

A corner of the Barat Day Nursery, Barat Settlement, where the Children of Mary sodality served the community

"Sacred Heart's commitment to community service served as the most formative aspect of my education. I felt uplifted by the experience of connecting with others on a human level and wanted to make it my life's work."

—BROOKE PICOTTE '87

Peggy McCall dressed for First Holy Communion, 1934

of tenements, and despite the renovation of the chapel, the idea of relocation was resurrected. Forty blocks to the north, famed financier Otto Kahn, senior partner at financial giant Kuhn, Loeb & Company, was also coping with the Depression. The 62-year-old Kahn's fortunes were not as disastrously impacted as so many others, but he and Mrs. Kahn had lost interest in entertaining, and they began to consider the sale of the magnificent, five-story neo-Roman mansion he had built at 1 East 91st Street.

Looking out over Fifth Avenue and the reservoir in Central Park across from it, Kahn's 74-room home was built in 1918 in part to house his extensive art collection. Appearing box-like from both 91st and Fifth Avenue, the building actually let in immense amounts of natural light through the Renaissance courtyard that hollowed out the back, or north side, of the house, and afforded views of the park over the stone balustrade.

On March 29, 1932, Mothers Levis and Padburg first walked into the hall of Kahn's mansion off 91st Street for a visit. After a brief tour, Mother Levis uttered the prophetic words, "We will someday live in this house."

Negotiations began immediately between the Convent, through Pease and Elliman, and Kahn, through the Oheka[4] Corporation, which represented Kahn's real estate interests. Almost immediately problems arose with restrictive covenants that stipulated that the building had to remain a private home. Subsequent discussions, which depended upon neighbors like the

---

4 Oheka was an acrononym taken from the name Otto Herman Kahn, and was also the name of Kahn's famous castle on Long Island, built the year after the mansion on 91st Street.

Madison Avenue school students, 1934

Otto Kahn had many ties to the arts and to early Hollywood. Artists and celebrities of the day were a common sight at 91st Street. Here is Otto Kahn with Douglas Fairbanks, Sr. and Charlie Chaplin at the studios during a visit to Hollywood in 1926.

Burdens in 7 East 91st Street next door and the Hammonds at 9 East 91st Street, were initially unproductive. It wasn't until the next year, 1933, that Oheka began to have success at removing the restrictions through its attorneys.

By 1934 the Reverend Mother Vicar put her hope in the hands of St. Joseph, according to an anonymous convent diary written during the time. "We prayed on, multiplying acts through the last solemn weeks of Lent—by this time our O.K. intention [for the Otto Kahn house] was being spoken of openly. Holy Week brought more prayer, more acts ... the air seemed bristling with the sparks of the fire so soon to blaze into the flame of accomplishment."

Mrs. Burden and her sister, Mrs. Hammond, were now working with Oheka, and the "following Monday, the transferred feast of the Annunciation," continued Mother Graham, "our prayers were answered. What seemed to be the last obstacle had been removed." Indeed, near the end of February an agreement was reached to trade the three brownstones on Madison Avenue plus $500,000 cash for the mansion at 91st Street.

A couple of weeks later, on St. Patrick's Day, March 17, the Superior Vicar, Mother Gertrude Bodkin, visited Madison Avenue and made the written observation that "the time seems to have come, in God's design, our intention is confided to Saint Joseph, and we hope to reopen the school in September in another quarter not too far from here."

Two weeks later, on Friday, March 30, Otto Kahn

was in his office when he suffered a heart attack and passed away in the room at 67 years of age.

"We were shocked to hear of the death of Otto Kahn, who had been stricken at lunch in his office," wrote Mother Graham. Candles were sent to the New York houses and Kenwood to burn at St. Joseph's altar for Wednesday of Easter week in prayer for the great financier and builder of Sacred Heart's new home on 91st Street.

PREPARATIONS FOR LEAVING

As the 1933–34 school year drew to a close, the 136 pupils—86 seniors (students in grades 9 thourgh 12) and 50 juniors (students in grades 1 through 8)—were told that the school would open at 91st Street the following fall. Preliminary papers transferring ownership were signed the first Friday in May, about five weeks after Mr. Kahn's death, though legal possession was deferred until June 8, presumably to allow the grieving Mrs. Kahn to remove her belongings.

Commencement occurred as usual, but it was both special and bittersweet, according to Mother Graham. "Our children seemed to catch the spirit of such a moment, and the keynote of the farewell address, expressing loyalty, voiced the sentiments of all, and stirred emotions poignant and sacred—it is their proud privilege to reproduce, amidst more stately surroundings, the spirit of simplicity and devotedness, characteristic of the children of Madison Avenue."

Once the school year was complete, attentions turned to the gargantuan task of transferring 50 years

"...the air seemed bristling with the sparks of the fire so soon to blaze into the flame of accomplishment."

Portrait of Otto Kahn

91st Street's bookplate, created by Sister Saida Hawkins in honor of the school's new home

of education—both material goods and long-standing traditions—50 blocks uptown. Fortunately, the Kahn home was deemed extraordinarily well-equipped to serve as a home to the cloistered nuns as well as to the 130-plus students. "Only the strictly necessary alterations are being made to conform to building regulations," wrote Mother Graham, "for we have a house admirably suited to our day school and one in which we shall be able to do much more for the glory of the Sacred Heart."

Preparing the library for the move was the first order of business. Each class pitched in, cataloguing the volumes in their homerooms. "Even the first Elementary tots claimed the duty of assisting Mother H. to catalogue their 'Honey Bunch' series, and similar ponderous literature," noted one diary. At the end of the summer in the Kahn library, Saida Hawkins, RSCJ, created a bookplate for the reorganized collection.

After that, everything was coordinated for a rapid move, because the location of the school on Madison Avenue meant that traffic could not be tied up for long periods of time. In mid-June two large vans arrived for packing, and "by the 22nd every piece of furniture, box, and article of any kind was decorated with a Morgan tag, the color of which indicated the floor it was to be carried to."

The actual move occurred between the 25th and the 27th of June. On the last day, as the Madison Avenue site was but a shell, Father Casey, Cardinal Hayes's secretary, notified Mother Graham that His Eminence the Cardinal, who had served the school as a priest years before, wanted to stop by Madison Avenue on his way to an appointment uptown. He stayed for

Among the cherished pictures,
That hang on
Memory's wall,
The one of the dear,
old Convent,
Seemeth the best
of all. (Adapted!)

A poem from the Madison Avenue school archives

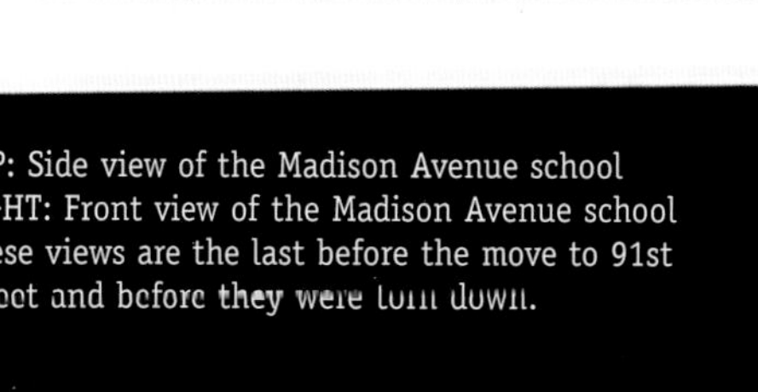

TOP: Side view of the Madison Avenue school
RIGHT: Front view of the Madison Avenue school
These views are the last before the move to 91st Street and before they were torn down.

REAL ESTATE

Sale of Kahn House Completed

Taken by Society of Sacred Heart for School in Exchange for Madison Corner.

The complete story of an important ... tion, which was disclo... action ...

THE NEW YORK SUN,

BUILDINGS IN KAHN REALTY DEAL

...th Ave.

...hn House ... esiden...

...rk Times.

CLASSIFIED ADVERTISEMENTS
Pages 5 to 17

Section 10 AND 11

1934. RE

STATELY FIFTH AVENUE RESIDENCE PURCHASED FOR SCHOOL.

KAHN SALE SHOWS TRENDS IN REALTY

Well-Known Mansion on Fifth Avenue Will Be Used for Girls' School.

TO GET TAX EXEMPTION

Court Action Needed to Modify Covenant Limiting Use of Site to Dwelling.

STABILITY IN LAND VALUE

Madison Avenue Property, Taken as Part Payment in Deal, Will Be Site of Taxpayer.

By L. E. COOPER.

Once more the errant trends in ...

...ORK HERALD TRIBUNE,

...actions in the C...

...n Dwelling ... Schoolhouse After June 1

Society of Sacred Heart Exchanges Madison Ave. Site for 5th Ave. Corner

Catholic Scho... Three W...

...KAHN HOME

Court Asked to Remove Re... strictions to Permit Use of ...th Av. Home as School.

...AL EXPECTED SOON

...gie and Others as Have Given Con... Judgment.

...ion through Pease & Elliman ...6 and decided on the ... 1932. Court actio... remove restri... property ar...

twenty minutes, greeting everyone amid the tagged boxes and rugless floors. "What memories must have passed through his mind," pondered Mother Graham, "of the days ... when he had been our confessor. The Cardinal strolled about the empty premises before blessing the nuns and their new venture and heading on his way."

THE BEGINNING AT 91ST STREET

In the first weeks, furnishings of all kinds, including a grand piano, arrived at 91st Street as the community pitched in to create a school out of a private house. The nine religious who moved in that August deemed themselves "happy as larks." The first reported gathering of the religious in the new location, with Reverend Mother Levis, and Mothers McNally, White, Blair, O'Rourke, O'Conner, Simpson, and Rainsford in attendance, was on August 25 (though the religious had been in the cloister all summer). On September 13th, just a week before the seniors were to arrive, a surprise—and more change—occurred when Reverend Mother Levis was reassigned.

"A great sacrifice has been asked of us by our Blessed Lord," wrote Mother Graham. "Our dear Mother Levis has been called by our very Rev. Mother General to the government of Overbrook." A few days later, her replacement, Mother Ellen Green, arrived.

The school year began with a diminished student body of 123, a reflection of a move to a new neighborhood to which some of the old families perhaps didn't wish to travel. The students who did make the switch reveled in their new surroundings.

Corner of 91st Street and 5th Avenue in the 1930s

> "For we have a house admirably suited to our day school and one in which we shall be able to do much more for the glory of the Sacred Heart."
>
> —MOTHER GRAHAM

Group of RSCJ on the roof of the Kahn Mansion

When the school moved to 91st Street, Mrs. Meany, who worked for the nuns for many years, termed it "a grand palace." In addition to the spacious new interior, the girls now enjoyed athletics in the wide open vistas of Central Park, where the city had created a hockey field in the East Meadow. Betty Sherwood arrived on October 1 to coach hockey practice Monday, Wednesday, and Thursday from 2:15 to 5 p.m., and competitions in both field hockey and basketball were scheduled with Kenwood, Overbrook, Eden Hall, Maplehurst, and even the Manhattanville College freshmen. Some of the latter were no doubt recent Sacred Heart alumnae and likely envious of their ex-classmates' new home.[5]

The first open house occurred on September 30, when about 125 parents, alumnae, and friends visited. A more formal opening ceremony occurred November 7 when Reverend Mother Green, Mother Patterson, Mother Hill, and Mother O'Connor welcomed 600 guests who came to look at the school and admire the numerous gifts of flowers, and even furniture, that had materialized before the event. Guests milled about the house and by 4:00 p.m. filed into the assembly hall to listen to music.

Mrs. Kahn herself visited that day to see how her old home was faring as a school for girls. "Mrs. Otto H. Kahn was so graciously accepted—her presence in our midst had a significance all its own," wrote Mother Graham. "When Mrs. Kahn stepped off the elevator she greeted her, and now our, engineer (Olsen) who was acting 'elevator boy' for the day." Before the day was over, the aged widow expressed great surprise at how

5 Six students from the Class of 1934 had entered Manhattanville.

View of Central Park from the Kahn Mansion roof

A view of the Kahn Mansion from Fifth Avenue, 1930s

suitable a convent and school she and her late husband had inadvertently built 18 years before. The entire event, filled with awed guests, music, singing, celebration, and excited students showing parents their new classrooms, was a proper christening for a wonderful home.

Over the next few years, the Kahn mansion at 91st Street would grow accustomed to the constant, pattering sound of hundreds of little feet and the swish of black robes as the Convent of the Sacred Heart at 91st Street increased its enrollment and built on the traditions of 50 years at Madison Avenue.

The aged widow expressed great surprise at how suitable a convent and school she and her late husband had inadvertently built.

A few students who transitioned from the Madison Avenue school to the 91st Street school

Ann Louise Heide '45

Elise McCully '45

Pat Duffy '45

as we pulled our toboggan! slowly up the long

CHAPTER 3

End of an Era

1934–1963

As Sacred Heart struggled to hold on through the Depression and adjusted to its new home, it faced additional problems stemming from the fact that, since the beginning of the century, fewer and fewer women were entering religious life. "The number of schools rose considerably," noted the Society in its history. "The enrollments rose enormously, while the number of workers rose hardly at all, [leading to] increased tension and overwork."

TOP: Mary Ranney and Helen Sweeney as young novices
BOTTOM: Mary Ranney, RSCJ, 1971, after the discontinuation of the habit

Mother Elizabeth White, Mistress General from 1932 to 1936, and Mother Mary McCarthy, who took over as Mistress General in 1936, met this lack of religious at 91st Street as Mistress Generals were doing all across the country: by hiring more and more lay teachers, a solution that put an increasing strain on an already meager budget. On the positive side, because they were not cloistered, the lay teachers could plan and oversee outings the religious could not.

Cardinal Eugenio Pacelli's visit to Manhattanville in 1936 represented the biggest event since the school's move to 91st Street. The Vatican Secretary of State and Camerlengo (a position analogous to chamberlain) was welcomed with a reception, to which the students of 91st Street traveled. "Mother White decided the regular uniforms with collars and cuffs were dowdy," said Isabelle Stricker Kelly '38, "so we were, to the horror of our mothers, dressed in blue silk with red piping." The visit grew in importance three years later when Cardinal Pacelli was elected Pope Pius XII.

The same year the white smoke ascended from the Sistine Chapel chimney for Cardinal Pacelli, 1939, Mother Mary Ranney arrived at 91st Street. As the longest-serving educator at 91st Street, Mother Ranney is considered by many to be the embodiment of the school in the twentieth century.

"I wore two caps," she says of those early days. "When I was at 91st Street in my first year I taught all six grades, but I spent a lot of time with the first grade and was head of the Lower School," a role from which she would finally retire nearly 30 years later,

Portrait of Mary Ranney, RSCJ in the chapel, 2002

What was the difference between THE MOTHER SUPERIOR AND THE MISTRESS GENERAL?

The Mother Superior, sometimes referred to as Reverend Mother, was responsible for the supervision and spiritual well-being of a particular house or convent and its school. She delegated the authority of running the daily life of the school to the Mistress General, who served in a similar capacity as today's head of school. Also accountable to the Mother Superior were the surveillantes, religious who were in charge of school activities, discipline, and student affairs, and the Mistress of Studies, who was responsible for teaching the faculty and for implementing the Plan of Studies.

in 1967, to become Mother Superior of the House for one year. She would officially retire from all duties at 91st Street a full 64 years later, at the age of 91, in 2003.

Barely five feet tall and possessed of a knowing twinkle in her eye, Mother Ranney not only became one of the most well-loved and respected teachers, but a mentor to faculty. "Mentoring is so important, and Mary was an excellent teacher of teachers," says Judy Brown, RSCJ, who taught with Mother Ranney in the 1960s. By the time Mother Ranney arrived, the shadow of the Depression had mostly lifted, but it had been replaced by the shadow of another war, at the hands of Germany's Third Reich, which was preparing to march on Europe. All those of the Jewish faith had already been forced to begin carrying identification, and the previous November had marked *Kristallnacht*, the night of broken glass in Germany and Austria, when over 25,000 people were rounded up and sent to prison and over 7,500 businesses and synagogues were destroyed, leaving no doubt that war was inevitable. America, exhausted by World War I and the Depression, simply wanted to stay out of the conflict.

By May of 1940, at the end of Mother Ranney's first year, the Society's attention was diverted from the burgeoning tragedy when the new Pope, so recent a visitor at Manhattanville, beatified Mother Philippine Duchesne, "a bright moment in the war" according to a Convent diary.

In that same year, the Convent began the Mother Duchesne Residence School, where students pursuing advanced coursework after high school graduation in

New York could both live at the Convent of the Sacred Heart and seek additional training and instruction. To house this new school, the Convent acquired the James A. and Florence Sloane Burden House next door at 7 East 91st Street. Built by Warren and Whetmore for the well-known steel magnate between 1902 and 1905, the Burden house is a 38-room mansion built in the Beaux-Arts style. Mrs. Burden, a great-granddaughter of Commodore Cornelius Vanderbilt, had entertained there lavishly, greeting guests such as Mark Twain and the composer Giacomo Puccini, at the base of the spectacular marble spiral staircase that ran for three floors, leading into the dining room, the ballroom, the library, and other spaces that would prove wonderfully suitable, as had the Kahn mansion, for the Convent's purposes.

ANOTHER WAR

The next year, on December 7, 1941, America's hopes for staying out of World War II evaporated with the attack on Pearl Harbor. Within ten days 91st Street held its first air raid drill, sending the entire community to the well-fortified basement of Mr. Kahn's stone mansion. In January, in a grim reminder that New York itself could soon be a battleground, first aid courses were begun. American troops throughout the country readied for European deployment, while at 91st Street hockey in the park was suspended and the field given over to Red Cross activities and social work. At the same time, refugees began appearing in the city, and tending to them and collecting supplies and funds for

Postcards showing the Alumnae Room and Club Room in the Duchesne Residence School

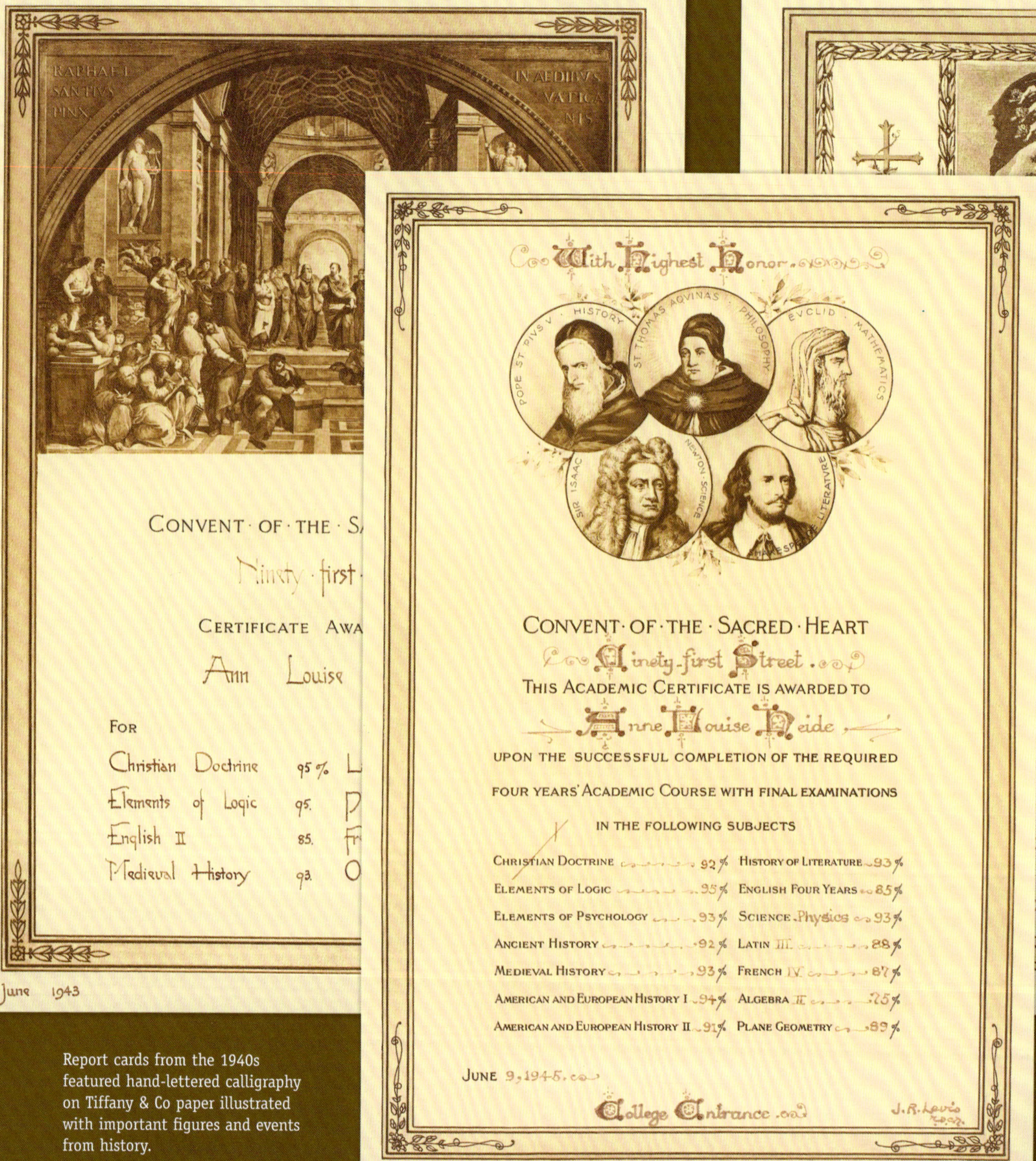

Report cards from the 1940s featured hand-lettered calligraphy on Tiffany & Co paper illustrated with important figures and events from history.

the war replaced traditional activities and spending for the Convent's missions.

Over the next several years, the shadow of the conflict in Europe hung over 91st Street just as it did over the rest of the city and the nation, and the school responded much as it had during the previous war. Mother Virginia Rainsford, the study hall surveillante, made certain the students supported the war effort with their voices by drilling them in the songs from the different military divisions. "Anchors Away," "The Caissons Go Rolling Along," and "From the Halls of Montezuma" regularly echoed through the corridors of the Kahn mansion, military hymns for the prayers for peace and the guns firing an ocean away on the front.

Despite the constant daily reminders of the war, the nuns endeavored to continue life at the Convent as normally as possible. In 1943, Mistress General Jane Saul, who was also spiritual director to the Children of Mary sodality and taught senior religion, struggled with the arrangement with the chaplains, complaining in her notes that "a different priest comes each week or each month, and we never know who is coming." And in 1944, the Convent received its first phone connection, though much discussion was held over where to put the device. Eventually one was placed in Mother Saul's office, and one in the outside hall, although it was only to be used for receiving messages, not conversation.

That same year, 1944, the Madeleine Sophie Retreat Group was formed "for the purpose of the sanctification of its members through the practice of the Annual

An early photo of the James Burden Mansion

The shadow of the conflict in Europe hung over 91st Street just as it did over the rest of the city and the nation.

Basketball Team

"The basketball players are whipping around the court, making baskets, making fouls and really having good times. Noroton was our first opponent of the season, and after a long and merry ride to the rolling hills of Connecticut, we bowed to the victors in an exciting game. Hopes are high, however, for the great rival—Eden Hall—who plan to stay for the weekend and share the gay times of we New Yorkers. St. Savior's then hails our team for the last grueling match of the season."

—Excerpted from 91st Street's 1946 yearbook

Retreat and other good works." And as the war drew to a close in 1945, missionaries from all over came to the Convent for a world missions symposium. Whether through the war or missions, the girls were being exposed to a large world outside their school and their small neighborhood in New York.

POSTWAR YEARS

Though no one knew it as the Armistice was signed, the 20 years between the end of World War II and Vatican II would represent the end of an era in all Sacred Heart schools as the church's efforts to modernize in the mid-1960s would eliminate some of the symbols and rituals that had come to represent a Sacred Heart education: the nuns' habits, the religious as the primary instructors, prîmes, ribbons, and other century-old practices.

In 1946, however, the school simply seemed to revert to happier prewar days. "We entered school each day through a side door on Fifth Avenue, which led us to our lockers on the lower level," wrote Martha Rowland '52. "In those days, the Convent still had a very distinctive French flavor. We never had snacks, we had goûter. We didn't have holidays, we had congés. We never played hide-and-go-seek, we played cache-cache."

Discipline remained the hallmark of every aspect of school life. "In my day," wrote Jane Barrett Cortellesi '52, "the school was one of structure. Choice was limited, but our curriculum tended toward the classics.

"Our class was composed of 14 students, and it was very quiet. We walked, always in a group, in silence from study hall to classroom. The highlight of the day … after goûter … was a game of cache-cache, where half of the members of the Upper School hid and the other half had to find them." Silence was required because it was thought to promote not only order but discipline. Talking was allowed during break time between 10:20 and 10:30 a.m., and on the way to lunch, but not at lunch.

"Most classes were small," agrees Maureen Meehan O'Leary '59, who entered the school in 1947, and whose mother, Miriam Fitzsimmons Meehan, had graduated in 1930. Unlike other schools, "where girls studied together, dressed in their own clothes, seated all day in the same classroom at blond-wood desks that held all their books, 91st Street was vastly different. When a student rang a loud bell in the corridor, we moved from classroom to classroom carrying our books: English with Mother Craig and religion with Mother Heide in homeroom, science with Mother Maginnis in the basement lab, ancient history with Mother McCormick in another classroom, math, French, Latin in yet other rooms.

"We never left our group unless given permission and were then escorted by a red-, green-, or blue-ribbon girl, chosen for her leadership qualities or because she knew her way around the school."

V.V. Harrison attended another Sacred Heart School, but like all Sacred Heart students everywhere, experienced the same traditions. In her book *Changing Habits*, she wrote that "there was a military crispness and pride in the performance of even the smallest chore. Ceremonies and feast wishes and … even games of cache-cache and

Goûter

Goûter, from the French "to taste," is a long-standing tradition in Sacred Heart schools. In the days of boarding schools, when it was not uncommon for classes to meet until 5 o'clock in the afternoon, it was necessary to provide students with a mid-afternoon snack. Later, as the schools grew, the cost and logistics of providing the daily goûter became too complex, and today goûter is a special treat to which students look forward on special feast days and holidays. The goûter tradition at 91st Street included a mother-daughter tea. Pictured below is Heartie Look '02 with her mother Jeanne Blatte.

Study Hall

What is now the Upper School library used to be the Upper School study hall. The surveillante would sit at a desk in the front of the room (which is facing west), toward the students, who were paired with "desk mates." Morning announcements and prayers were made in the study hall each day, and students took vicariates (three-hour exams) and studied in the room in the afternoons. A code of absolute silence was enforced.

field hockey were executed with a learned precision. Nothing was done to excess. Every aspect of Sacred Heart life was carefully practiced and beautifully orchestrated."

A DEDICATED FACULTY

Despite dwindling numbers, the RSCJ remained the heart and soul of the school in these postwar years, and numerous teachers made an indelible impression on the students.

While everyone had their favorites, one thing was certain: the RSCJ were all well qualified. "The nuns were intelligent and knowledgeable," says Jane Cortellesi. "I can remember talking to someone who was a docent at the Metropolitan Museum of Art, and she said Mother So-and-So at 91st Street knows more about Greek archeology than I will ever know."

Mother Saul, in addition to being a highly competent administrator, was a particularly progressive teacher of senior religion. "To this day I have not had another religion class that could compare to hers," wrote Cecilia Camargo Monturo '45. "In that class we were encouraged to read writers of other faiths, to compare, discuss, and discern. We read books like *The Screwtape Letters* and *Perelandra* by C.S. Lewis. She challenged all of us to develop our minds and not be afraid of expressing opinions on controversial topics .... Mother Saul was our Vatican II in 1945. She was way ahead of her time."

In 1951, thirteen years after Mother Ranney's arrival, another RSCJ, Mother Angela Bayo, came to teach fifth grade. She returned to Kenwood for her master's degree, then came back to 91st Street in 1956 to teach ninth grade English history, Latin and French and serve as the surveillante of the Upper School. Always even-tempered and nurturing, Mother Bayo followed a rule of "never scolding a child while angry."

Coming with Mother Bayo in 1951 as the new Mistress General, succeeding Jane Saul, was Mother Cora Brady, who "wore her stripes lightly and administered well," according to Frederica Kane Fissell '52. As the teacher of senior religion, "she spoke to us of Charles Péguy and Pierre Teilhard de Chardin.... She never sat; she paced, she swooped, or she stood: eyes shut, hands clasped, on the very brink of Ascension."

Like Mothers Ranney and Bayo and so many other teachers at 91st Street over the years, Mother Brady used her academic subjects as springboard topics for deeper matters she wanted her students to ponder. "One afternoon she undertook to explain to us the notion of evil as an absence of good," wrote Cecilia Carmargo Monturo. "'Who made this hole? Who made this nothingness?' She laughed often; not at us, not with us really, but perhaps a hint at the glorious absurdity of the human condition."

Indeed, for most of the faculty, learning was exceedingly important, but it was also a means to an end. Sacred Heart was not educating girls to be able to hold their own conversationally on the cocktail circuit or at their husbands' business gatherings, but to respond to the world in their own way and to make an impact on it in some positive fashion. And that required character building, not only in discipline but in self-awareness, in knowing themselves and their capabilities.

"She challenged all of us to develop our minds and not be afraid of expressing opinions on controversial topics."

—CECILIA CARMARGO MONTURO '45

Mistress General Jane Saul

Angela Bayo, RSCJ, in 1969 and in 1971, after the discontinuation of the formal habit

"You can be yourself, who you are; that was one of Mother Sophie's original ideas," says Jane Reynolds Andrews, who graduated from Elmhurst in 1962 but, like all Sacred Heart students, experienced the same spirit and traditions as those at 91st Street. "Each child's gifts and personalities are hers alone, and she is trained to be the best she can be. It's very individual. A Sacred Heart school takes care of the mind and the soul."

In this spirit, questions like Mother Brady's about good and evil were asked, and answers were expected to the larger questions of life. Opportunities were taken to cast mundane matters into larger, more existential terms. The answers weren't as important as the activity of thinking, of struggling both alone and in community with larger issues. In that way, every child, by learning her best way to contribute to the world around her, would be the single child for whom Mother Barat founded the Society.

ACADEMICS AND AWARDS

The curriculum, particularly in regard to the social sciences, continued to evolve innovatively and was ahead of most other schools in the way in which it was presented, demanding the girls think in global terms.

"When I went on to Newton College, a Sacred Heart college in Boston," remembers Maureen O'Leary, "they had instituted two years of study of Western culture in which faculty from all different disciplines came in, and everything was interdisciplinary. It was quite new at the time in 1959, but it was so Sacred Heart to me, because that's the way the curriculum was organized

Portrait of Angela Bayo, RSCJ, 2002

First Fridays

First Fridays in the Sacred Heart tradition were celebrated with special religious observances. The entire school would celebrate a morning Mass, followed by breakfast. In the afternoon there was a procession complete with a guard of honor, made up of students chosen to carry a banner and wear special sashes. The procession included Benediction, singing traditional Sacred Heart hymns, and a collection for the missions.

at 91st Street. The history, English, logic, philosophy... I came out with such a love of learning, because everything was related."

Still, there were strengths and weaknesses. "I think that the academics when I was here were very strong in certain areas," she continues, "but math and science were far weaker than today. We had general science, and I think there was physics one year for a couple of kids, and biology."

Every year feast days were celebrated in honor of Reverend Mother and the Mistress General. A formal address, composed by one or several students, would be presented, usually by one of the blue ribbon girls, in the presence of the entire student body. These feast day addresses provided opportunities for public speaking. Each student's best written work (called "feast work") would be put in a binder and put on display in the library. In the afternoon there was a musical presentation or some other kind of entertainment. Many alumnae have held that after enduring so many oral exams and speech days, "any Sacred Heart woman can talk to strangers."

The traditions that had been in place for over a century at Sacred Heart schools continued to maintain their high level of performance. Prîmes, the Monday assembly, remained as central to school life as academics. "Even more important than the Bien cards were ribbons," wrote V.V. Harrison, "which were awarded to students who achieved special merit: blue for the upper classes (grades eleven and twelve), green for grades nine and ten, narrower green for the Middle School, and pink and red in the Lower School. All ribbons were voted on by the students, ratified by the religious and awarded at a special ceremony at the beginning, middle, and end of the school year. Each student knelt in front of Reverend Mother as the coveted grosgrain sash was affixed over her right shoulder. To be a Ribbon was an honor sought by many but achieved by few."

Outside of academics, students of the Sacred Heart "were required to participate in a variety of extracurricular activities," remembers Harrison. "Along with the prescribed hour of sports in the afternoons, there were classes in letter writing, music, sewing, diction, and even politeness. Each in its own way reflected the Catholic approach and was designed to balance the moral, physical, and spiritual aspects of student life and ultimately to produce well-integrated feminine personalities."

THE SOCIETY, NEW CHALLENGES, NEW MISSIONS

All through the 1950s, the suburban migration every city was experiencing, New York included, began to have a deleterious effect on many urban schools. At Sacred Heart the student body ranged from about 230 to 250, but the junior school had been decreasing in size since 1947, a result, analyses showed, of "young marrieds" moving out of the city. Compounding this problem was a stricture against large classes, which limited enrollment. "We cannot accept more than 25 in a class without special permission from the Reverend Mother Vicar," wrote Mother Brady in her journal in 1953. The small class size was fine for academics, but

Field Day

Field Day is a long-standing tradition at schools of the Sacred Heart. As this photo from the late 1950s illustrates, the outing to the Greenwich campus for a day of athletic competition and fun is something 91st Street students (and faculty) have enjoyed for many years. Joan Carter McHugh '59 and Linda Kelly Hodgen '59 (above) remind us that school uniforms may change, but placing an importance on athletic activity does not.

Study Hall, 1952

with the lay faculty stretching budgets, more students were needed.

In 1954, partially to offset the attrition in the student enrollment, the kindergarten was started, but as the numbers remained roughly the same, the new class merely served to keep the overall enrollment level for the first several years of its existence.

Finances continued to be a challenge. "A large secular staff is a tremendous financial drain but seems necessary," wrote a superior in her diary in the 1950s. Extracurricular activities "seem valuable for the formation of the children, but they put extra pressure on the young mistresses." The school wanted to create more space and considered building onto the roof, but found the cost to be prohibitive. In short, the squeeze was tightening, so two measures were begun around 1960: increasing tuition and increasing enrollment.

ADMINISTRATIVE CHANGES

In 1946, Marie-Therese de Lescure was elected Superior General. Reverend Mother De Lescure, who would visit 91st Street in 1953, would begin her own modernization process five years later by revising the Plan of Studies and the School Rule. The Spirit and Plan of Studies, published in 1958, sought to establish an international uniformity of spirit, rather than a specific curriculum, for a Sacred Heart education, giving much more autonomy to each school and even to the individual classroom teacher.

Reverend Mother de Lescure was succeeded by Sabine de Valon, who emphasized more missionary

VIRGINIA CURRY
1942 – 1953

LUCELLE DALLY
1943 – 1953

MARY ANN COLEMAN
1943 – 1953

MARCIA FENNELLY
1942 – 1953

JUDY GARSON
1949 – 1953

MICHELLE O'SHEA
1941 – 1953

Graduation photos of the era had a distinctive look.

Superior General Sabine de Valon at 91st Street with a student dressed in period costume

projects. Three years after de Valon took charge, 91st Street was supporting, with other Sacred Heart institutions, "four missions in Japan, one in Korea, one in Formosa, two in India, two in Egypt, four in the Congo," according to Mother M.L. Shroen, Mother Superior from 1959 to 1962. "Moreover, this year we have opened a fifth house in northern Japan, one for the outcasts in India, and are opening a normal training school in Uganda, Central Africa, in January. Also, we are opening a house in Caracas, Venezuela."

With the increasing involvement of parents in the life of the school, a Parents Committee was formally organized in 1962, under the leadership of Mrs. Peter Flanigan. It described itself as a "public relations group through whom both contact and assistance for the school might be improved." Goals were set to increase endowment and scholarships, and to raise funds for expansion and teaching aids, and while their involvement would be helpful in an upcoming fundraising effort, it would be another ten years before this group would become an association and the vital component of the community that it is today.

MORE THAN AN EDUCATION

Between the Depression and Vatican II, 91st Street stayed true to its ultimate mission of educating young women in mind, body, and spirit while its approach to that task necessarily evolved with the rest of the world.

The changes involved an increasing number of lay teachers, a new plan of studies, a new kindergarten, and new concerns with both missions and the threat

Students from the Lower School on the rooftop in 1952

What was the COMMITTEE OF GAMES?

In 1952, long before the creation of the school athletic department, Sacred Heart sports thrived under the guidance of the Committee of Games, a student group that had certain responsibilities for sports and teams at 91st Street. The committee coordinated a number of intramural activities and all student teams, including hockey and basketball, which competed with other New York independent schools and with Sacred Heart academies out of town.

ABOVE (FROM LEFT TO RIGHT): Marcia Fennelly, Lucelle Daly, Martha Murphy, Ruth Ann Gimbernat, Margaret Bermingham, Dorothy Hosford, Rica Kane

of communism. But in the early 1960s, despite accommodations to a changing world, Madeleine Sophie Barat, had she arrived at the doorstep of 91st Street, would have recognized the school as distinctly "Sacred Heart" both in terms of the religious in the halls and the rigor of the studies.

Mostly she would have recognized the school because the focus had always remained not only on educating its students, but, more importantly, on providing them a deeper sense of spirituality, a deeper sense of being cared for, and a deeper sense of awareness of and commitment to the problems of the world at large than can be found in books.

"How cloistered they were and how protected we were," reflects Maureen O'Leary, "and yet there was an incredibly strong but subtle message that 'you are intelligent women and girls.' In those days you were raised for marriage. They didn't challenge that message overtly, but everybody understood on a subliminal level —which was then articulated a lot later—that you should 'use your mind, be a person within the world.'"

Kandy Shuman Stroud '59 remembers a motto from her days at 91st Street that sheds light on these observations. "'A man's head and a woman's heart'" she says, "The nuns meant us to be every bit as good as a man intellectually, to develop as a whole person, and I think not competing with boys in the classroom was useful. By the time you entered the business world you were accustomed to succeeding, because in your own right you were used to responsibility."

But the development of capable women at 91st Street and other Sacred Heart schools was still a byproduct of an even deeper agenda, which was creating in students not only a practical and intellectual capability to hold their own in society, but a spiritual and moral sense of obligation to use those capabilities to contribute to the world at large.

"I developed a level of confidence in my education, and I learned how to articulate my passions and interests, because I was given the opportunity to do so at Sacred Heart."

—KIM TAYLOR-THOMPSON '73

NEW SPIRIT AND *Plan of Studies*

In 1958, a document entitled the Spirit and Plan of Studies deliberately set aside the details of a syllabus and the rigid adherence to a single program method first established by the Society's Plan of Studies, by trying to convey the spirit of a Sacred Heart education, which would remain consistent despite external changes brought about by time and circumstance. In this spirit, American schools adapted their programs and methods to suit the special situation of each school, and the formulation of the first Goals and Criteria for Sacred Heart Schools in the United States (1975) provided a shared articulation of the principles and values of a Sacred Heart education.

CHAPTER 4

A Window Opens On 91st Street

1963–1967

By the time Mother Judy Brown arrived from Noroton as surveillante at 91st Street in 1962, the various cultural revolutions that would sweep the world and, in particular, the Catholic Church, the Society of the Sacred Heart, and the Convent at 91st Street, were just getting under way.

By that year, President Kennedy had already committed the first 400 Green Beret "advisers" to Vietnam. By the mid-1960s, however, the increasingly unpopular conflict would mushroom to become the first televised war, stimulating a peace movement that would spawn demonstrations across America and the world. This movement would merge with the counterculture—the hippies and eventually the entire "Woodstock nation"—that was coming out of California to redefine lifestyle possibilities for all American youth, including the impressionable young girls at 91st Street.

Two other groups were taking stands in the early 1960s that would also have an impact on the Convent of the Sacred Heart: civil rights demonstrators were challenging America's segregation with marches throughout the South, and women, inspired by Betty Friedan's seminal book, *The Feminine Mystique*, began to demand a greater respect and equality.

The Catholic Church had, although somewhat unknowingly, begun its own revolution as early as 1959 with the election of Angelo Giuseppe Roncalli as Pope John XXIII. Within a few months of being named pontiff, Pope John announced, "I want to throw open the windows of the Church so that we can see out and the people can see in," stating that he intended to convene what would become known as the Second Vatican Council.

As the Council evolved from its first session in the fall of 1962 to its last in December of 1965, it seemed to tap into, or at least parallel, the spirit of cultural revolution which was sweeping the Western world. The 16 documents that emerged from the meetings represented not only a massive social teaching, but also a major shift toward modernization. John XXIII

Students in recreation

died in 1963, well before the Council's conclusion, but on October 28, 1965, his successor, Pope Paul VI, issued a decree on the adaptation and renewal of religious life that would have reverberations not only down to each parish and priest, but to every Sacred Heart school, including 91st Street.

Known as *Perfectae Caritatis*, the decree seemed on the surface to be more sensible than revolutionary. "The manner of living, praying, and working should be suitably adapted everywhere," it said, "but especially in mission territories, to the modern physical and psychological circumstances of the members and also, as required by the nature of each institute, to the necessities of the apostolate, the demands of culture, and social and economic circumstances."

In fact, in stating simply that it was time for the church to enter into the modern world, *Perfectae Caritatis* opened the way for the modern world to rush into the Catholic Church and into every parish, mission, and school across the world. The Convent at 91st Street, like all Catholic institutions, would never be the same.

In the early 1960s, immediately prior to this flood of change, 91st Street fluctuated between 300 and 334 students, with about 100 students in the Upper School. Tuition hovered around $750 for the Lower School and $1,200 for the Upper School. Eighty percent of the faculty were religious. In 1961 Mother Ursula McAughon was turning over the role of Mistress General to Mother Peggy Brown, and a year later, Mother Marie Louise Schroen would cede the role of Mother Superior to Mother Margaret Shea, who had been Mother Superior once

As the religious came out of the cloister they participated in all aspects of the modern world.

"I want to throw open the windows of the Church so that we can see out and the people can see in."

—POPE JOHN XXIII

Mother Maragret Shea, RSCJ, with students

" The Sacred Heart nuns were incredibly accomplished. Many held multiple degrees. They were bright, interesting people to know."

—CATHERINE CURRY '70

before, from 1953 to 1958. Mother Krim oversaw the Duchesne Residence School next door at 7 East 91st Street.

At that time, says Sister Judy Brown, "there were still plans of study, developed, further refined, and disseminated so that every country was following that course. The meetings took place under the guidance of the mother house. The plan was a printed book .... We had periodic visits from provincials who would visit classes and comment, and from the Director of Studies who would come like an avenging angel and cut you off at the feet if you weren't doing a good job. Then we had a local director of studies."

Catherine Curry '70 entered the first academic, or ninth grade, in 1966, just after the Second Vatican Council concluded. Though she found the system rigid, she also found it refreshingly rigorous.

"It was very different, on many levels, from the parochial school I had attended," she says. "The biggest change was intellectual. For instance, the approach to religion was much less doctrinal. At parochial school we had a very strict catechism. At Sacred Heart we studied Hinduism, Buddhism, and the philosophy of religion. The Sacred Heart nuns were incredibly accomplished. Many held multiple degrees. They were bright, interesting people to know."

The give and take of ideas between students and teachers was also a new experience. "Since I was eight years old, I had learned that you don't speak until spoken to, and so I kept my hand down. You gave only objective answers. Then at Sacred Heart I was suddenly in small classes and encouraged to speak. I was so quiet, though, by training, that on one report card they wrote, 'Why

The Change From MOTHERS TO SISTERS

Members of the Society have used a number of titles over the course of its history. During the nineteenth century "Madame" as a term of address was used because the Society had come into existence shortly after the French Revolution, when it was not always possible to obtain recognition under a specifically religious name. "Madame" was later dropped, and members of the Society became known as Mother or Sister. Why were some members called Sister and others Mother? Like many women's religious orders, the Society before Vatican II had a hierarchical structure of membership. Upon entering the Society, a woman became a member of one of two groups. Those who undertook domestic duties, crucial for the daily running of the house, were called coadjutrix sisters (sometimes referred to in other orders as lay sisters). Those who undertook teaching and administrative duties were called choir religious because they sang the Divine Office, the community prayer. Choir religious usually had two and a half years of study upon entering the order, including instruction in the Society's constitution, spiritual exercises and reading, and teacher training. Coadjutrix religious immediately began work and usually did not receive additional study or training. Choir religious were referred to as Mother and coadjutrix religious as Sister; they usually lived quite separate lives within the house, but as Janet Erskine Stuart wrote, "We know that we could not do without each other." After Vatican II, however, these distinctions were eliminated, and by 1967 all members of the Society took on the title of Sister.

Sister Atkinson

Students continue a tradition of decorating the school for the Christmas holiday, 1960s.

doesn't she speak up more?' It turned out to be a big and liberating transition."

The biggest difference Cathy Curry felt, though, was in the love from the nuns. "Even on the very day they took us around, before my first day of school, they were warm and welcoming. That was the biggest difference: the love that was behind every teacher, in every class."

Sister Bayo (for as part of the change all Mothers became Sisters), who took over for Sister Ranney as Head of the Lower School in 1967, exemplified this aspect of a Sacred Heart education for many. "It is such a sacred trust," she reflected back on her career, "to be given the responsibility to help these children grow into the unique persons that they are. It is important to value the mind and intellect, but the heart as well. It is important for children to know they are loved, and that their mistakes aren't the end of the world."

Part of this love was communicated in the security that the RSCJ community provided: They were always there at 91st Street, in the cloister, always in their habits, always dedicated first and foremost to the children. Then suddenly, one day in January of 1967, the window in the Catholic Church that John XXIII had spoken of cracked just a little and let the first breeze of the world into the previously calm stone interior of the old Kahn mansion. On that day the nuns' habits were modified from the severe bonnet to a more streamlined, off-the-face version.

"When the change from the habit to secular dress occurred," remembers Sister Ranney, "the Superior said, 'I would like you, the three heads of school, to change to the new habits on Friday.' The other nuns would change Monday. This was to help the students accommodate gradually to the change." Eventually, of course, even the modified habits gave way to conventional clothing.

While she was Head of the Lower School, Sister Ranney bore the enviable and time-honored task of greeting and shaking hands with every student every morning as they came to school, and that is where her charges first encountered the difference. "I was on the fourth floor every morning saying 'good morning' to them. One child ran up to shake hands and said, 'Where is Mother Ranney?' She didn't recognize me." Nor had she been able to switch over to calling her "Sister."

At least in appearance, and to the distress of some, after 1967 the secular and the religious became all but indistinguishable in the hallways at 91st Street and all other Sacred Heart schools.

VENTURING OUT INTO THE WORLD

Though it was highly visible, the elimination of the habit represented only a symbol of far more fundamental and far-reaching changes. The first of these involved the removal of the cloister and the encouragement to the religious to move out into the community. "Our directives were all rewritten," remembers Sister Ranney. "We were given cautious permission and cautious direction to go out into the world. The leadership was quite worried we would lose the spirit of cloister, the spirit of contemplation and worship that we of

Sister Ranney carrying on the tradition of greeting students in the morning, 2002

course all wanted to maintain. But when it started, it increasingly snowballed."

The religious were suddenly free to socialize, eat at restaurants, visit museums they had never seen, despite having lived around the corner from them for decades. At best it was a double-edged sword. On one hand, according to Sister Ranney, the change was more than a breath of fresh air in that it added a dimension to their role as educators, but it also proved to be a surprising challenge to parents. "It was wonderful for me because I saw students and parents at a whole other level, but sometimes it was hard for the parents because they felt a lot of their lives had been hidden from us, and now we were out there and could see the real thing."

Sister Judy Brown agrees. "I experienced parents who had a sense of betrayal because we were no longer their mothers behind the cloistered wall in the long graceful habit with the fluted bonnet and sitting peacefully in the parlor or in our offices talking to them when they came. All of a sudden we were in secular dress going out to meetings with our friends. I think they found it unsettling."

V.V. Harrison, in *Changing Habits*, saw the change across the order and recognized in some cases a melding with the emerging trends of the day. "It appeared that the carefully-sewn fabric of the well-ordered life was beginning to unravel. Many Sacred Heart nuns, anxious to explore their newfound freedom, joined with the children they were teaching in testing the social trends and in some cases the fashions of the soaring 60s."

Just as all this was occurring, the Duchesne School, in operation since 1940 as a two-year program for

A view from the roof of the Kahn Mansion

high school graduates with specialties in social and secretarial skills and early childhood education—the only finishing school on the Sacred Heart roster—ran into problems with accreditation. "Some of our graduates wanted to go on to four-year colleges," says Sister Bayo, "but their courses at Duchesne were not always accepted for credit." In 1966, as a result of these accreditation problems, the Duchesne Residence School closed and the Middle School made plans to move into the Burden House, creating welcome room in the very cramped Kahn Mansion.

As radical as it all seemed, the disappearance of the habit, the cloister, and the Duchesne Residence School represented, in Sister Bayo's words, "only the tip of the iceberg." The biggest sea change the order would face involved a new choice of vocations. For the first time in history the RSCJ were not only allowed to go out into the world, but even encouraged to find other vocations beyond academia. With fewer and fewer women entering the religious life, and now the remaining ones either leaving the order because they did not like the changes or leaving the schools for new fields, it is easy to see how the balance of teachers swung quickly, over a period of just a few years, from religious to lay.

"Many were leaving because they couldn't take the changes," says Sister Ranney, "then we lost some because we weren't changing quickly enough. We lost some wonderful religious in the late 60s. Some of our order left the schools and went into ministries serving the poor, or ministries with social justice."

Green and Buff

Intramural competition has a long history in Sacred Heart schools. At 91st Street the friendly rivalry has always been between the Green and Buff teams. Students were placed on a team when they entered the Upper School and remained on that team for the rest of their Sacred Heart career. Students participated in a variety of competitions throughout the year, including field hockey and cache-cache (hide-and-seek) on congé, culminating in Field Day. This picture from February 1965 shows a basketball game between the Third Academic class (juniors) against the Fourth Academic class (seniors). According to the caption on the photo, the juniors "always win. The 4th did not have a chance!"

"Until 1967," said Beatrice Brennan, Mistress General from 1954 to 1958, "we religious imparted a world vision to our students within the confines of a cloistered life ... fed by a combination of wide reading, lively imagination, news from abroad, the presence in our schools of children from all five continents, and a few practical efforts to help where help was needed.

"But in 1967 cloister was removed from all apostolic congregations. It became possible to live in small communities not only within or near our schools, but in low income neighborhoods as well, all over the world. I decided to give it a try." Brennan spent a number of years in small villages along the Nile in Egypt, before returning to work at a social service agency in East Harlem, where she served as a liaison helping parents negotiate the public school system.

While more adaptive than the alumnae or parents to the changes after the initial shock of seeing the nuns in secular dress, the students were not immune to the stresses of the day. "Almost overnight they changed," says Cathy Curry. "It was radical and very sudden and yet they still needed to go out to people to help them. As a student it was disruptive, because a lot of people were uncertain what they should be doing, and some clearly didn't want to teach, but wanted to pursue more social justice issues. It was a time of trying to find out what their role should be. They were incredibly brave and intellectually honest about what they were doing."

In their search, many of the nuns faced dissatisfaction from parents and alumnae. "Right after the change," says Sister Ranney, "I was on a bus and a woman came and sat next to me. I realized she was an old Child of

Mary, a sodality of the Sacred Heart, and she looked at me and said, 'You, too?' in a very disdainful way.

"And I said, 'Yes, me too.' She was very distressed that I was in contemporary dress. I said to her, 'Madam, I've taught your children for ten years and I've never once questioned any decision your family made for your children, and now I ask you not to question the decisions my family is making for me.' She took it nicely."

CHANGE UPON CHANGE

In the midst of all these changes came another that many found even more unsettling. The New York province had made a decision to diversify the student bodies of Sacred Heart schools with more African-American and Latin American students, and Sister Peggy Brown and Sister Ranney offered 91st Street as a pilot program. In 1964, June Murray became the first African-American student at 91st Street. As the program developed, there was far more diversity than ever before. Most were students recruited from schools in upper Manhattan and entered in the ninth grade.

There were, in fact, larger cultural issues at play, beyond the fallout from Vatican II or even the civil rights movement, which rendered the late 1960s a difficult time for independent schools all over the country. In short, the counterculture was gaining more and more currency. Private schooling, as representative of the establishment, was quite simply becoming less and less fashionable among some people, and many schools were suffering declining enrollments. Many schools could have weathered a temporary downturn,

TOP: Students taking exams in the ballroom, 1965
BOTTOM: Students having dinner in the ballroom, 1965

but when the early 1970s brought challenging economic times, rendering public schools even more attractive alternatives for financial reasons, many closed their doors.

At numerous Sacred Heart schools, the situation was even more dire than at their secular counterparts, for in addition to facing the same deleterious social trends as everyone else, the schools faced additional financial challenges. With all the Vatican II changes, many parents were pulling their children out because they were, for the first time since Madeleine Sophie Barat founded the order well over a century before, uncertain of their school's direction. Combined with the fact that more and more lay teachers with comparatively higher salaries were taking the place of the disappearing religious, Sacred Heart schools around the nation were faced with dramatic budgetary shortfalls.

"It came like lightning," one of the older nuns recollects of the school closures in *Changing Habits*. "Most of us really had no idea. It seems the order hired a professional consulting firm to evaluate Sacred Heart schools across the country. They looked to the future and saw that there were not going to be very many vocations, that the focus of new vocations was drawing away from teaching.... Anyway, they decided that the best thing to do would be to consolidate some of the schools and close the rest."

The first round of closings began in 1968, and over the next five or six years, nearly a dozen schools were closed. Noroton in Connecticut, Elmhurst in Rhode Island, Eden Hall in Philadelphia, Clifton in Cincinnati, Grosse Pointe in Michigan, and St. Joseph's School for Boys in Menlo Park were just a few of the Sacred Heart

Noroton

From 1925 to 1972, the Convent of the Sacred Heart in Noroton, Connecticut, whose alumnae are now part of the 91st Street community, maintained the tradition of Sacred Heart education in a setting of sweeping natural majesty. Pictured below is the school's brick terrace, looking out onto the field hockey field and, beyond that, Long Island Sound. One interesting feature of the field was that it was necessary to circumnavigate a tree growing in the middle of the grounds, very much a home field advantage for Noroton athletes.

NOROTON SCRAPBOOK

schools to shut down in the wake of change.

"In many cases there wasn't a future ... there wasn't a clientele," says Sister Judy Garson, head of Noroton School when it shut its doors in 1972. "For instance, Noroton simply had to close. There was no way to keep it open." In order to maintain Sacred Heart ties, the alumnae of the closed schools were "adopted" by some of the schools that were spared. Ninety-first Street became the new home for the over 1,000 Noroton alumnae in the mid-1970s, keeping them connected to the Sacred Heart tradition and to each other.

Ninety-first Street weathered this storm and continued to try to build for the future, uncertain though it was. Opportunity came from an unexpected quarter when the Duchesne School closed in 1966. The nuns took it as God closing one door and opening another. The Burden mansion was now available, but it was a time of significant financial challenge, so they decided to embark on an uncharacteristic path: they appealed for $90,000 in renovations.

The Très Bien Ball was held to support expansion, and in the end, from special events and solicitations by the parents committee and others, the school received over $150,000, proving that 91st Street retained a united and resilient community. The Middle School moved in, and the additional space in the Kahn mansion was utilized with an eye to expanding the student body.

"There is something inexplicable about this community of closeness and warmth, comfort and nurture, that can offer friendships so close."

—ETKIN CHAMOGLU '03

Duchesne students on an outing

The teaching of the class mistress is the first factor in the mental training given. It requires, however, the personal reaction of each pupil, and the exchange of ideas. The enthusiasm of all must be contributed to their mutual progress. Thus each child is a vital and active element in the class. The classroom is a home; the children love it. They may even decorate it themselves sometimes, as the year goes by, and thus give to it a character which will show the progress of their scholastic activities.
Exactitude, order and silence are essential for serious work. Each one, with the help of the mistresses, imposes this control upon herself, in the interests of others, own work and still more in the interests of her for the good of the whole.
10
IV
MORAL FORMATION
Moral training is a preparation for life in
future. The education given at the Sacred H
at forming true personalities, characters s
well-rounded.
NOVENA OF CONFIDENCE
St. Madeleine Sophie in her later years.
7
6
SPECIAL DEVOTIONS
MANUAL OF PRAYERS
AT
SACRED

CHAPTER 5

Setting A New Course

1967–1980

If there was a particular high-water mark of the cultural revolution in America, it was 1968. The broad spectrum of events—and extraordinary contradictions—of the day can be gleaned from the fact that both Martin Luther King, Jr. and Robert Kennedy were assassinated just before what was termed the summer of love. The Woodstock rock concert in a farmer's field in New York and the tragic National Guard shootings on the campus of Kent State University were

TOP: Sister Joan Kirby in the 1970s
BOTTOM: Sister Joan Kirby at Sister Salisbury's memorial, 2005

both a year or two in the future, but students and African-Americans were both rioting, women were demonstrating for equality, and hippies were having love-ins. On the political front, Senator Eugene McCarthy had emerged as a presidential candidate to give an establishment voice to the peace movement, virtually driving President Lyndon Johnson out of the race and setting Richard Nixon up to defeat the Democratic nominee, Hubert Humphrey, in November.

In that fall, a new Mistress General, Sister Joan Kirby, arrived from the Stuart Country Day School of the Sacred Heart in Princeton, New Jersey, which had been started only five years before. It had been the last school the order opened before the closings began a few years later.

Sister Kirby was "a scholar and a wonderful teacher," says Sister Judy Garson, then a colleague from Princeton. "She could relate to all constituencies and is a woman of enormous integrity, great truthfulness, and someone the parents could trust." She was, in other words, exactly what 91st Street needed at the time.

"When I arrived," says Sister Kirby, "it was a time of enormous upheaval. There was a certain amount of resentment that nuns were moving out of schools, and there was not a very deep understanding of what we were doing."

The larger issue, and one with which she was well equipped to deal as a competent administrator, remained the lack of any significant vehicle to communicate about the changes to the school's various constituencies. Parent-teacher relationships at 91st Street had always been informal, one-to-one, and until Vatican II brought in so many changes, there had been little need for newsletters or other forms of mass communication. Consequently, many parents heard about changes in uniform, behavior, or new teachers by word of mouth —usually from their children or other parents.

"The school was an entity unto itself," says Sister Kirby. "It had been cloistered, and we did not generate much official communication with alumnae and parents. It was no fault of theirs. Lack of communication was a function of our lifestyle. It was simply the way we operated at that time."

Looking beyond communications, she notes, "We ran the school and answered to the provincial, who was responsible to Rome. We were interiorized. Consequently, there was no organized parents association. We rarely had to raise money or look for students." So, she says, "the true supporters began to rally around. Jane O'Connell '59, then a parent, said, 'You need a parents association,' and she was right. Jane was the first official Parents Association President, and she did a magnificent job of bringing parents to school and communicating what it was about."

"Lots of things were in transition," says Jane O'Connell, "and the Parents Association was a product of the shift from religious to lay teachers. There were pieces that were needed that weren't needed before. It was clear that the role of parents in the school's life was changing, and we needed to address those changes. I proposed a parents association to help organize and direct the parents' efforts, and everybody said, 'Of course.' So in the mid-1970s, Mimi O'Hagan and I put the bylaws together, and from the beginning, we emphasized the

Portrait of Sister Joan Kirby in the 1960s

Cafeteria

Prior to its relocation across the hallway in the No. 1 basement, the student cafeteria was housed in what is today the Lower and Middle School gymnasium. Known officially as the "refectory," this particular dining room was specific to Upper School students at tables of six. Meals were prepared by the nuns, and each table included a designated head, usually a student from the 4th academic (12th grade), and a mix of students from the Upper School grades. This rotating system engendered community between the various grade levels. During their Lenten retreat, however, students observed a code of silence throughout lunch, and a spiritual book was read aloud during the meal.

need for us to take our role in the community as seriously as possible. As a result, it became a requirement that the PA president would be a full member of the board of trustees."

Sister Kirby also asked alumna Mimi O'Hagan, Eden Hall '47, a public relations executive, to lend her considerable organizational skills to an effort to better address the needs of the alumnae by creating an alumnae board to lead the already established alumnae association. "Sister Kirby was headmistress when she asked me if I would join the alumnae board," she remembers. "I got very involved with the alumnae in the 1970s, first serving as the alumnae president, then working half-time in the development office."

The alumnae, as galvanized by O'Hagan and others, represented a critical piece of the puzzle. "We realized no one was going into religious life anymore; women had more choices, vocations were down. Little by little the religious were going away. The question was, 'How are we going to carry on this mission?' The obvious answer was the alumnae, because they know it, they've lived it, and they've experienced it. This education is a gift from one generation to the next. You have to ensure it, or it is not going to be here."

Admissions was another area of concern in the early 1970s. Greater diversity was important to the mission, but attracting the right students and getting out the true Sacred Heart message during times of uncertainty and change was critical. Zonni Hume Edmondson, Noroton '48, arrived to serve as admissions director. "Zonni turned admissions around," says Sister Kirby, "by reflecting what the school was really about."

Advancement had gained a certain foothold with the drive that had raised $150,000 to revitalize the Burden Mansion. "The development office had several skilled people," said Jane O'Connell. "They were pretty good at putting things together; there was an alumnae office which wasn't sophisticated but had an address list. There was an annual fund, but no capital campaign." But in the face of great financial challenges, a changing faculty, and new structures and traditions, much more advancement infrastructure was needed.

AN OUTSTANDING FACULTY

Despite the turmoil of the times, there was much to be encouraged about even before all the administrative changes took hold. Perhaps most importantly, a changing faculty did not mean a diminished faculty.

At the time Sister Kirby took control, religious such as Sister Ranney, Sister Bayo, and Sister Brown remained on staff and mostly in leadership positions, but by then 60% of the faculty were lay teachers. "We not only had lay women and men, but a variety of religious backgrounds," says Sister Brown.

In fact, many of the teachers who would anchor the faculty for the next several decades at 91st Street started to arrive in the late 1960s. Long-serving teachers, such as Kay Hines, Margo Mead, and Lovella Beres began teaching at 91st Street at this time, helping to develop the academic rigor that continued to emerge in all the three divisions. "We had so many good people," remembers Sister Brown, "such as Mary Jemail (then Mary Brady). She dates back to 1965, and like the

TOP LEFT: Sister Judy Brown, 1971
TOP RIGHT: Lovella Beres, 1971
BOTTOM RIGHT: Kay Hines, 1971

Mimi O'Hagan, 2002

TOP LEFT: Mary Jemail
TOP RIGHT: Jim Ward
BOTTOM LEFT: Margo Mead
BOTTOM RIGHT: Sister Eleanor Fox

religious, she was teaching her charges about far more than the subject at hand or the material in the text. She taught them about life."

Elizabeth Cascella Auran '78, who remembers Brady as "one of the finest teachers I've ever had," describes her "potent wit and that vibrant, even wicked laugh ... a firm integrity coupled with an offbeat flair and the way she appeared to know about absolutely everything." Mary Brady's classes were also collaborative, interactive, and dynamic, and she was known for delighting her students by inserting them into stories and lessons in order to heighten their interest. "Mrs. Brady was encouraging us to speak out and to take chances. [She] showed us the connection between literature and life, between truth and beauty, but at the same time taught us not to fear paradox nor the complex young women we were becoming."

Art teacher Margo Mead had arrived in 1965 and not only taught studio art in the school's basement studio, but engaged students at a very early age in the study of women artists, subtly expanding their horizons of what was possible in their own lives. When the students learned about impressionism in French class, reported an article in *Les Amies*, "Mead taught her students about the lives of strong female impressionist painters like Berthe Morisot and Mary Cassat, giving them articles to read about the artists, even in 4th grade."

Jim Ward was another of the great educators at Sacred Heart, and he bore the twin burdens of being a lay teacher and a male. In 1970, Ward had what amounted to a chance conversation with Sister Kirby one day in the front hall, and to his great surprise, she called the following day to offer him the position of head of the Upper School. He originally turned down the job. His reticence was no match for the concerted prayers of the RSCJ, and he accepted the position, came to 91st Street, and stayed for nearly two decades.

If the nuns were mothers, Jim Ward, tall, refined, and handsome, was certainly a father figure to many—a "father, a confidante, a friend, someone we could always count on," according to Pilar Cano '85. Ward had never before taught in a girls' school; he gained his footing quickly, however, and developed his own term for the deeper, spiritual agenda of a Sacred Heart school, the one that went beyond books to the heart and soul of a student. He called it the "hidden curriculum."

"He was a man who made each young lady in the Upper School feel as though her problem, her triumph, her day was the only one on his mind," remembered Laura McKenna Mazzaro '83.

Sister Eleanor Fox had one of the most dynamic and well-respected classes in the school. Her *New York Times* class, in which the only text was the daily *New York Times*, had "a profound impact," said Ellen McCurley '77. Sister Fox's class was a place in particular where students were encouraged to ask, interpret, and understand. The fact that the subject matter involved events happening that day, in that city, increased the relevance, and it was one of the most respected classes in the school. "By semester's end," said Nora Huber '69, "Eleanor Fox had armed the willing and attentive for philosophical and political combat."

Upper School student government, 1969

"[Mrs. Brady] showed us the connection between literature and life, between truth and beauty, but at the same time taught us not to fear paradox nor the complex young women we were becoming."

—ELIZABETH CASCELLA AURAN '78

REACHING OUT

Many joined in the effort to connect the students to the world at large from different perspectives. The opportunities to move into the larger community, and to bring some of that community in the form of economic and social diversity among the student body into the increasingly less insular convent, also brought greater awareness of the outside world. For example, in March of 1967, the school service program was expanded, and seniors, as part of a training for Christian living, were required to perform some form of community service every week, at a time and place of their choosing. One popular location was the Yorkville Youth Council Program, where more than 30 girls would contribute their time alongside students from other private schools in the area.

"We felt our commitment to social action was of extreme importance in Sacred Heart education," says Sister Kirby, who found she sometimes had to push the non-academic agenda to make certain it received enough attention. "Faculty sometimes felt they needed every minute for teaching, but it's really important to have students aware of commitment beyond the self."

Since the early 1960s Mimi O'Hagan had looked out even further than the surrounding community. She felt very strongly that, as an international order, the Sacred Heart schools had an opportunity, if not an obligation, to foster an international dialogue and understanding among the many students and alumnae scattered across the globe.

"In 1966 when I was a young woman with my own PR firm, I wrote to Rome and said that there was an

Some of the students from the sophmore class of 1971

opportunity to tap into international exchange through study or vacation exchanges. I asked if I could start a summer program. I took out a loan in 1967, brought 30 Americans from convent schools to France to live for six weeks in French homes of Sacred Heart students, then returned with 60 French teenagers, who stayed all over the eastern part of the U.S.

"We pushed the exchange idea very hard during the student year, and Madame Ethelee Hahn, head of the foreign language department, was asked by Sister Kirby to encourage these programs. There have been numerous international exchanges since then."

THE NETWORK IS BORN

As the Convent addressed the financial challenges of the late 1960s and early 1970s, selling the building and re-establishing the school in a space with less expensive maintenance was always an option to be considered. This idea, however, distressed historians and neighbors who were fearful that a developer would replace the Kahn and Burden mansions with an unattractive, light- and view-blocking high rise. Unfortunately, a designation as a historical landmark, which would have protected the buildings from being razed no matter who owned them, would have required the school to expend extraordinary funds in maintenance. Faced with this kind of continual expense and oversight, the school fought the designation for years.

Finally, in 1974, at the height of administrative changes and curricular expansion, a solution was reached with an interest-free loan that would allow the Convent

TOP: Mrs. Olive De Silva with her students
BOTTOM: Sr. Rosemary Roney reading to students

to maintain the property according to landmark strictures without an undue financial burden. In that year both the Kahn and Burden mansions were designated New York City historical landmarks.

While 91st Street, both the school and the building, had survived, the Sacred Heart schools as a group had changed immeasurably. For those that survived, maintaining the mission into the future continued to be a source of concern. If the RSCJ no longer dominated the faculty, and would be diminished even further as time went on, then, many asked, "What would make an institution a Sacred Heart school?" How would Madeleine Sophie's mission be maintained if there were no one from the order there to perpetuate it?

Jane Maggin was a 1965 graduate of Manhattanville and acting president of Manhattanville while her daughter attended 91st Street. "There were multiple provinces run differently," says Maggin, referring to the then five U.S provinces. "There were different rules for each group of schools. The Plan of Studies was gone, the old rules were gone," a set of events Maggin compares to a divestiture. "They had to do something, but the nuns were in unfamiliar territory. We needed an organization."

The answer, says Sister Garson, was in the "enormous lay involvement" that the remaining schools enjoyed. "The lay people we asked to work so closely with us wanted to be sure there would continue to be Sacred Heart schools. That was the cry everywhere. Whatever this was, we had to put it in a new language and develop strategies and methodologies. Over the years we had begun to have conferences bringing together lay faculty to develop a sense of family. Now we began to form the Network."

Sister Katherine Collins, Director of Education in the New York and Washington Provinces, was asked by the InterProvincial Board of the Five Provinces to expand her duties to include all the schools in the United States. "Kit was very much ahead of her time, and led us all," says Sister Garson.

The process involved a series of Stuart conferences, named after Janet Erskine Stuart, Superior General in the early 20th century. These conferences began as early as 1968 and established the first real dialogue and networking across the country between the lay and the religious educators.

At a Stuart Conference at John Carroll University in Cleveland, Ohio, in 1974, all the Sacred Heart headmistresses determined a need to define the essence of a Sacred Heart education. "There was lots of work to convey the sense and spirit," says Garson, "to capture what was so special about a Sacred Heart education. Kit helped us work it out. It was a hugely collaborative process."

The Network offered new opportunities for both the facutly and staff. "The Network began to develop workshops on Sacred Heart education and formation to mission," says Jane Maggin, "and also provided information about different positions thoughout the many Network schools."

Still, the Network remained a mere administrative structure until the first Goals and Criteria were finalized, an effort that recognized the fact that the RSCJ were disappearing, and that a need consequently existed to

Erin Flanagan '85 and Pilar Cano '85 at play

> "We tried to capture the spirit in the Goals and Criteria, which is so much more than learning doctrine about your religion. It's about the whole spiritual development ... the development of the heart."
>
> **—SISTER JOAN KIRBY, RSCJ**

Jane Maggin, 2006

Jane O'Connell, 1987

articulate, record, and pass down the principles of a Sacred Heart education. "We tried to capture the spirit in the Goals and Criteria," says Joan Kirby, "which is so much more than learning doctrine about your religion. It's about the whole spiritual development ... the development of the heart. That is part of what we hoped for for our students."

They were written down because, as the preamble to the Goals and Criteria stated, "values taken for granted or left unarticulated become inoperative." The Goals in 1975 centered around five ideas:

1. The relevance of faith in a secularized world
2. A deep respect for intellectual values
3. A social awareness which impels to action
4. The building of a community as a Christian value
5. More personal growth in an atmosphere of wise freedom

More than anything else in the last 30 years, it has been the Goals and Criteria which people have understood to have embodied the spirit and the mission of a Sacred Heart school. No lay educator, having read the document, can fail to understand the extraordinary scope of their duty beyond the classroom. "For anybody that comes here to teach, part of their contract is a commitment to the Goals and Criteria," says former Alumnae Board President Jane Reynolds Andrews. "It is the verbalization of the way in which I and every Sacred Heart student was educated. It was unspoken in the old days but it was there. Now, those who want to be here, to be part of this community, must embrace the Goals and Criteria."

Board of TRUSTEES

In 1976, 91st Street converted to lay leadership in the form of a board of trustees. Since its first meeting, the board had included at least three members of the Society of the Religious of the Sacred Heart, and the presence of alumnae on the board has grown steadily over the last 30 years years, as is evident in this picture of the 2004–2005 board. From the very first board to its more recent groups, trustees have shared a dedication to Sacred Heart and its mission as expressed through their hard work and generosity.

FIRST BOARD OF TRUSTEES

BOARD OF TRUSTEES 2004–2005

The Board had expanded and included 13 Alumnae members in 2004 FRONT ROW: Mary Hart '87; Barbara Rogers, RSCJ, Elmhurst '70, Manhattanville '74; Laurette Bryan, Eden Hall '65, Newton College '69; Ann M. Conroy, RSCJ, Manhattanville '47 BACK ROW: Adele Reilly Grant '71; Angela Bayo, RSCJ, Greenwich '44, Manhattanville '48; Brooke Picotte '87; Paula Toner, RSCJ, Manhattanville '65; Mary De Luca de Bourbon '64; Cathy Curry '70; Jane C. Maggin, Manhattanville '65; Maureen Meehan O'Leary '59, Newton College '63; Diana Barrett '62

Once developed, the Goals and Criteria created additional issues of accountability and enforcement. "It was not enough to say 'have Goals and Criteria,' " says Sister Garson. "We had to have a whole methodology worked out, a whole system for evaluation."

Each school is evaluated every five years by an evaluation group appointed by the provincial. This evaluation was not to focus on the quality of the educational offerings, which state accreditation addresses, but how successfully the school is adhering to the Goals and Criteria.

In 1990, under the leadership of Sister Susan Maxwell, the Executive Director of the Network, the Network of Sacred Heart Schools was established as an independent entity. It was formed as a membership corporation; the members are the board chairs, the heads of schools, and the Provincial team. Jane Maggin was the founding Board Chair and suggests that "the real and symbolic start of the Network as an independent organization gave real credence to the commitment to Sacred Heart education for generations to come."

TRUSTEES

By bonding together, the schools that comprised the Network of Sacred Heart Schools had provided their own clarity after years of uncertainty following Vatican II. But in simply providing a mission and a set of guidelines while leaving execution up to the individual schools, management remained an issue. This was resolved by developing formal boards of trustees charged with oversight of the schools; however, accountability for the Goals and Criteria continued to be the responsibility of the Province.

Sister Kirby had a leg up on this step. After recruiting tremendous support from alumnae, parents, and new hires to strengthen alumnae, fundraising, and other areas, she then built an advisory board which would eventually be the Board of Trustees. "We stabilized those areas and then developed the first advisory board with Crocker Nevin, Mary "Frisky" Fuger Hickey, and John Felleman. They were all incredibly supportive. It was advisory to begin with because the nuns hadn't yet relinquished control."

BUDGET CRISIS

The efforts of the late 1960s in regard to space and enrollment had worked to the extent that the student body approached 400 by the end of the decade. Unfortunately, increasing expenses of paying more lay teachers and a dip in enrollments in the mid-1970s created yet another budget crunch.

One of the solutions Sister Kirby and the newly formed board of trustees arrived at involved divesting the Convent of some assets that may have been good ideas originally, but which had become albatrosses. "We had bought two brownstones on 92nd Street to expand," says Sister Kirby. "Halfway through the decade, though, we were facing a major financial crisis because they were a serious drain with their mortgage payments. They were sitting there unused while enrollment was going down."

Sacrifices were being made all around. Some faculty and staff volunteered to go for months without taking

A few recent chairs of the Board of Trustees
TOP LEFT: Emily K. Rafferty '67
TOP RIGHT: Mary Anne Boyd
BOTTOM LEFT: Vincent T. Pica II
BOTTOM RIGHT: Cornelia Thornburgh

CHAIRS OF THE BOARD OF TRUSTEES

John M. Felleman, 1976–1979
Alfred Y. Morgan III, 1979–1982
Winthrop Rutherfurd, Jr., 1982–1986
Richard Winfield, 1987–1990
Terrence Schwab, 1990–1993
Emily K. Rafferty, 1993–1997
Mary Anne Boyd, 1997–2000
Hilary Adams, 2000–2001
Vincent T. Pica II, 2001–2004
Laurette Bryan, 2004
Jane Maggin, 2005
Cornelia Thornburgh, 2005–

a paycheck, so it was time to make more serious changes. "I remember clearly sitting in a meeting and saying 'we're going to turn this around,'" says Sister Kirby. They did it by selling the brownstones, which not only cut the budget, but provided a large cash infusion.

A DECADE OF DEFINITION

By the late 1970s, the Vietnam War was over. The sagging economy of 1973–74 had revived. Watergate had mushroomed and receded. The struggles for equality continued, but the conflict that had marked the early days of the civil rights and women's movements had subsided. Some private schools were even coming back into favor, and enrollments had started to climb once more across the country.

At the same time, the Society had changed with the times. After the unsettling period of the 1960s, after change that would permanently alter the makeup of a Sacred Heart education, the Sacred Heart schools were forced in the 1970s to define themselves for the new educators who would carry the mission into the future. The Network now provided an organizational umbrella, and the Goals and Criteria a compass that helped leaders articulate the mission, which a decade before was perhaps written only in their hearts.

On 91st Street, the Convent of the Sacred Heart had also changed. Trustees now had oversight of the financial side of the school. New administrators ran it. It had survived because of a dedicated core faculty of religious who remained, such as Sister Ranney and Sister Bayo; new faculty who assumed the Sacred Heart mantle

TOP: Miss Cogan, in the midst of rapidly pirouetting young students in the Duchesne Hall
MIDDLE: Student's First Communion in the 1970s
BOTTOM: Student with class pet guinea pig

as their own; and a group of dedicated volunteers who put their shoulders to the wheel to help strengthen alumnae affairs, development, parents associations, and public relations. And finally, it survived because the right leader, Sister Joan Kirby, arrived with the right set of skills to establish a firm footing in a new time.

School trip to the Metropolitan Museum of Art, 1971

"The leadership, dedication, and patience of so many educators helped me to cope with an ever changing world, and ultimately to bring up my own children with a strong set of Christian values. To this day, when I try to explain to my husband and children what the Sacred Heart experience is, I simply use the word love."

—DEBRA DIMARCO '77

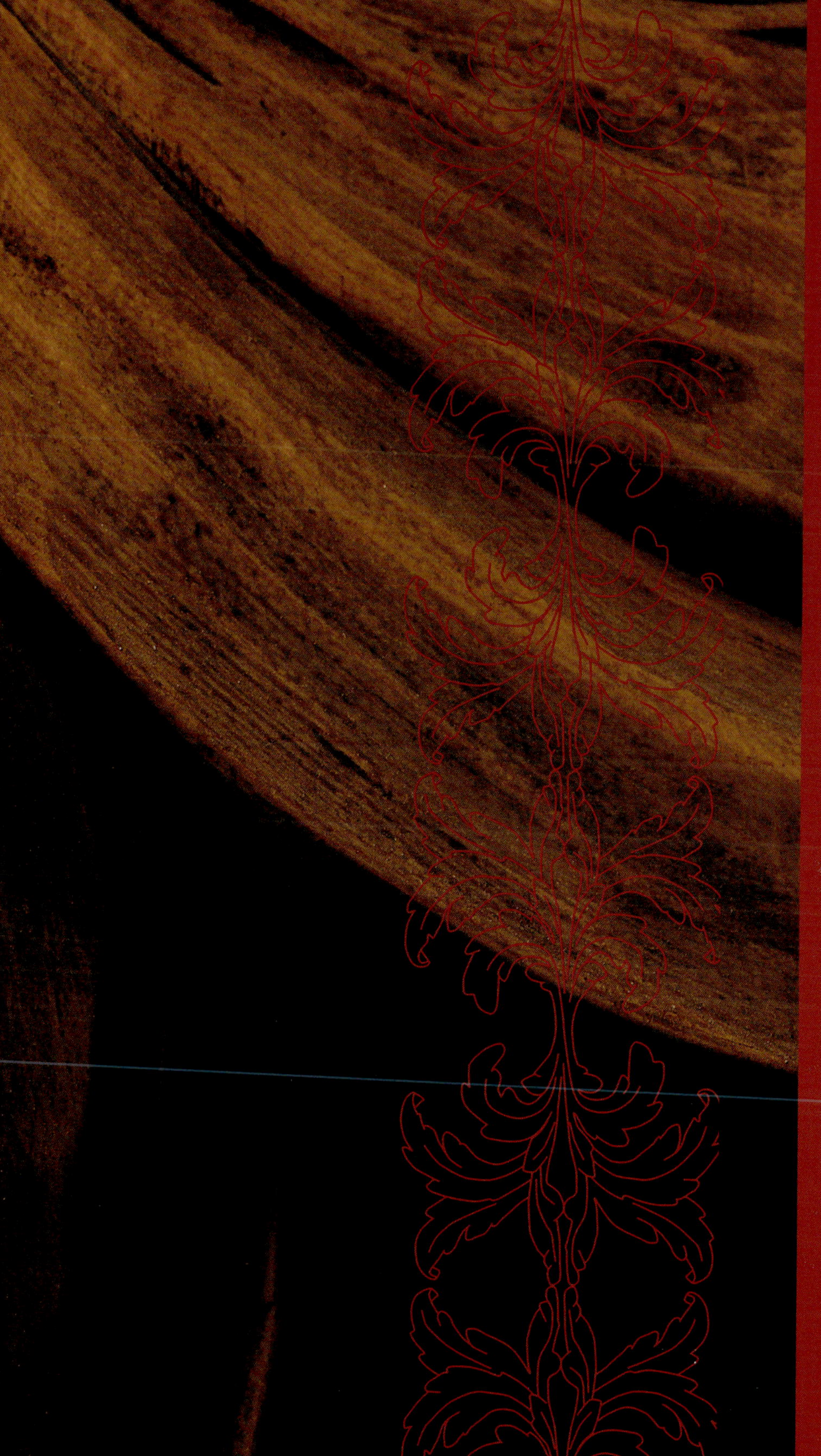

CHAPTER 6

The Defining Years

1980–2000

When Sister Joan Kirby announced her planned departure in 1979, the relatively new board of trustees did not have to look far for a replacement: just an hour up the road at the Convent of the Sacred Heart in Greenwich, Connecticut, where Sister Nancy Salisbury was headmistress. Sister Salisbury had been at four Sacred Heart schools, including 91st Street, since entering the Society in 1952 and possessed

Portrait of Sister Nancy Salisbury, RSCJ, in 1999

degrees in sociology, philosophy, history, and mathematics from Manhattanville College and the University of Detroit. By the time she had become a headmistress at Greenwich, she had gained a reputation as an excellent teacher, an extraordinary administrator, and a woman who had, in the words of Rosemary Sheehan, RSCJ, head of the Upper School at Greenwich, "the ability to listen with a sympathetic and discerning ear."

In fact, those who knew Nancy Salisbury claimed that her personal attributes in fact outshone even her extraordinary academic and administrative ones, and suggested that her unique mix of personal and professional skills was exactly what was needed for a school that sought to deliver a spiritually based, values-centered education of the highest quality.

Sister Eleanor Fox, who had been a student at Manhattanville with Sister Salisbury fifteen years before, once noted that "Nancy was always on the lookout for the one lone wolf or the underdog, or just anyone within her purview who might not be perfectly at home or at ease. I remember her approaching me to try to persuade me to join the group of regular student bridge-players, not because they needed me, but because she wanted to draw me into a social group. Nancy's outstanding character trait was her genuine love for people of every kind." Sister Salisbury's best friend, the former Mistress General at 91st Street, Sister Peggy Brown, felt strongly that Nancy would "make sure that there would always be a Sacred Heart school in New York," and implored her to take the position.

In September of 1980, Sister Nancy Salisbury became the second headmistress, or the 25th head of school if you count Mistress Generals, at New York's oldest independent school for girls.

THE SECOND CENTURY BEGINS

Sister Salisbury arrived at the beginning of one of the biggest celebrations in the history of the school. Founded in 1881, the school was about to enjoy its centennial year and embark on its second hundred years.

"The school's Centennial Year opened with a beautiful Liturgy at Saint Ignatius Loyola Church on The Feast of the Immaculate Conception, December 8, 1980," reported *Les Amies*, the alumnae news magazine. Various celebrations, special events, and academic contests marked the next twelve months.

The year-long celebration culminated on Tuesday, December 8, 1981, at four o'clock when everyone traveled downtown—in a torrential downpour that did nothing to dampen the spirits of the day—for a Centennial Mass celebrated by a dozen priest-friends of the school, at St. Patrick's Cathedral. Terence Cardinal Cooke was the celebrant, and Provincial Anne Conroy, RSCJ, and other dignitaries filled the nave. Afterwards, everyone returned to the Kahn and Burden mansions, which were opened all day for activities, exhibits, and parties. "It was one massive celebration," remembers Jane Maggin. "Parties in the hallways, parties in the ballroom. Senators, everybody. It was a big deal."

"I carried a banner down the aisle," said Caroline Samsen Mueller '83, a junior at the time. "I remember the awe and the magnificence of it and being in the church. It was a sacred event."

TOP: Sister Nancy Salisbury in the early 1980s
BOTTOM: Sister Nancy Salisbury with students, 1986

The Creative Arts Festival in the spring of the centennial celebration

"It was one massive celebration. Parties in the hallways, parties in the ballroom. Senators, everybody. It was a big deal."

—JANE MAGGIN

The Centennial was barely over when, in January of 1982, the Society in America decided to streamline its administrative structure by merging the five U.S. provinces into one, based in St. Louis. The entire order in the United States now operated under one provincial.

The National Commission on Goals (NCOG), a committee appointed by the Provincial, was also beginning a set of evaluations for all Sacred Heart schools. After some preliminary evaluations in the 1970s, the evaluation committee, consisting of seven members, both religious and lay educators, had formally started in 1980 with Villa Duchesne in St. Louis and Bloomfield Hills in Michigan. Ninety-first Street was scheduled for evaluation in 1983-84. Therefore, as soon as Sister Salisbury had taken office, the school began "working to develop the entire school program in the spirit of strong Sacred Heart education as expressed in the Goals and Criteria."

Sister Kirby had left 91st Street well prepared for such an evaluation, or, as Sister Salisbury said, as "fertile soil for growth." As a result of the administrative foundation Sister Kirby had built, Sister Salisbury had the luxury of focusing her attention more squarely on education.

In this regard, the task for English, history, and the arts involved maintaining 91st Street's typically high standards. As a forward-thinker who was in step with the larger culture, however, Sister Salisbury recognized that the girls at the 91st Street, like all girls everywhere, needed more encouragement and opportunities in the fields of science and math, and she set about raising their profile in the curriculum

The Dad-Daughter Dynamic

For over 25 years, Sacred Heart has celebrated its father-daughter traditions. As seen in this photograph of the 1981 Father-Daughter Dinner Dance, taken in 91st Street's centennial year, fathers and daughters enjoy the bonding that comes with Sacred Heart events designed exclusively to focus on this very special and unique relationship. Today the Dads and Daughters Committee is part of the Parents Association and sponsors a number of events throughout the year, including a boat cruise, a halloween party, and a theater outing.

Miss Conroy's second grade class, 1982

Sister Salisbury recognized that the girls at 91st Street, like all girls everywhere, needed more encouragement and opportunities in the fields of science and math.

and through improved programs and, eventually, better facilities.

By 1982, students were participating in numerous outside science programs, including internship programs at Cornell University Medical Center, New York University Medical Center, and Columbia University's Saturday Science Honors Program. Science director June McDermott noted that the goals of the overall science program involved "making the girls scientifically literate. We want to have an appreciation for all the sciences. We don't want the girls to be shortchanged in any one of them." Standard science courses—botany, biology, oceanography—were buttressed for 11th and 12th graders by studies in genetic engineering and recombination.

Beyond academics, service programs were explicitly central to the Goals and Criteria, as stated in the third goal: "a social awareness which impels to action." Significant advances had already been initiated in the late 1970s in this regard. For instance, to fulfill the 10th grade religion requirement, an intensive field work and reflection program combined service work with discussion sections with adults and other classmates. In other words, social awareness not only impelled to action, but the reverse was also implemented: action was used as an educational tool to further social awareness. Similarly, 11th and 12th graders not only performed weekly service, but could take a winter course entitled "Social Services in New York City."

The social program "takes personal strengths and moves them forward," notes Carolyn Carey Morey '91, one of five sisters to attend Sacred Heart over a period

Upper School students in the library

Bells

In 1989, the sound of Sacred Heart changed. Since the school's beginning the religious had used traditional brass school bells to mark the end of classes during the day. Each sister would have a turn at "handbell duty," ringing to indicate when students should move to their next class. In later years, another bell system was added to facilitate communication between the nuns. Because for many years telephones were not commonly available in classrooms and offices, the call bell assigned a unique combination of sounds to each sister so that she might know if she were being summoned to meet a visitor or take a phone call. According to *Les Amies*, "Sacred Heart has sounded slightly like a department store with the beep, beep, beep of the call bell system which seemed to call someone every two minutes." In 1989, the call bells and the general use of the handbell were eliminated.

of 30 years. "It helps build maturity and confidence. I worked at Sloan-Kettering once a week with two friends doing whatever the hospital needed of us. Another year we worked at Mary Manning Walsh Nursing Home, usually reading to residents. Other students went to Hall House to work with drug-addicted babies."

The program, she notes, started with the very youngest girls. "A fourth grader wouldn't leave the building, but she would help the kindergarten class with art work or be a big sister. Each year they exposed you to a little more. You were always taught to think beyond yourself and to determine how you can give back to the community. It develops the person and keeps them from getting too self-absorbed. There were also trips with other schools, like going to an orphanage in Belize."

In 1980–81, students also took greater ownership of the service component when a small group of 11th and 12th graders was formed to actually monitor, assess, and plan service work. By 1982 eighth graders were undertaking service projects in groups of six at different establishments such as Boys' Harbor Afterschool Program or Sister Leontine O'Gorman's Storefront Tutoring Program, and older girls were developing individual projects with a Service Coordinator. Some ventured off-campus several times a year for special programs outside the city.

REFURBISHING THE BUILDING AND BUILDING THE FUNDS

As Sister Kirby had revamped and strengthened the administrative structure, and Sister Salisbury was working to bolster academic areas that had traditionally been weak, it became evident that a third leg of the stool —the physical plant—also needed significant attention. The ballroom on the 3rd floor of the Burden mansion had been restored in 1976, the assembly hall at the Kahn mansion turned into a theater, and the stonework in the front hall had been cleaned and repaired, but fifty years had taken their toll on the mansions in many deeper ways.

"[Board chair] Win Rutherford asked me what the condition of the building was," says Jane O'Connell, then director of administrative services. "I said, 'It's falling apart,' and Nancy Salisbury agreed."

A subsequent planning study in 1984 noted that the cost of being a landmark had come home to roost. "Repairs made to these buildings are problematic. Most schools are not historic landmarks with ballrooms, murals, frescoes, or thick slate roofs, which were once highly prized. Few plumbers or workmen have the skills and the interest to work on historic buildings with mysterious plumbing, hard-to-locate electrical wiring, and impenetrable stone walls." As a result, during years of meager finances, basic maintenance had been deferred.

In the spring of 1984, architects Buttrick White and Burtis developed the school's first plan for refurbishing, renewal, and re-allocation of space. It was a multimillion dollar effort that would represent the first step in a long-range, multi-year plan focusing primarily on the roofs, heating systems, and plumbing. Work was begun after approval from the Landmark Preservation Commission.

TOP: Students with an early computer
BOTTOM: Marc Rosner with students in science class

TOP: School newspaper staff of *Spirit of 91*, 1984. LEFT TO RIGHT: Patricia Eva Oppenheimer, Audrey Choi, Teresa Wilson, Heather Zorn, Tila Newbery, Elizabeth Sullivan
BOTTOM: Students receiving the School of Excellence Award, 1991

Not long after the refurbishing began, therefore, plans were laid for another capital campaign. The Second Century Fund, a $3 million capital campaign, was publicly announced in 1988 with $1.2 million already donated. The Campaign reached the halfway point by the summer of 1989, and $3 million by the spring of 1991.

The $3 million raised through the campaign not only helped underwrite some of the refurbishment of the building, but met some additional, equally critical needs by putting some of the funds into the endowment. These funds created more opportunities for the faculty to study, travel, and work on projects during the summer or to gain extra training in new technologies. And it helped meet the upward push on salaries.

Campaign funds also underwrote continued progress in the priority areas of science and math by supporting a new five-year plan for the sciences, begun in 1991. This plan called for a shifting emphasis from life sciences to the physical sciences, additional offerings to guarantee that each student would take both chemistry and physics, and the addition of Advanced Placement (AP) courses in these same two subjects.

BASIC ACADEMICS REMAIN STRONG

Traditional education was certainly not forgotten through the mid-1980s and into the 1990s. In fact, in 1991, 91st Street was honored by the United States Department of Education with a National School of Excellence Award. Only 222 schools nationwide—18 in New York State —received the broad commendation, which included leadership, teaching environment, academic programs, student involvement and achievement, parent and community support, and organizational vitality.

The English department, among other departments, had helped to garner this success, as it had added three interesting new courses to the Upper School curriculum. Gundega Spencer taught an innovative, year-long elective world literature course focusing on African, Middle Eastern, and Asian work. The text she used, which was also used at some of the top colleges, was the first to integrate fiction, poetry, and drama in the same book. English department chair Elizabeth Poreba and teacher Jane Sperling also developed new electives in journalism and African-American literature, and seniors could take guided study with Katherine Hardison.

History, another stalwart of the curriculum, maintained its excellence through this period with department chair Sister Eleanor Fox, Ian Humphreys, a practicing archaeologist as well as a social studies teacher, and Gundega Spencer, whose history course complemented her world literature offerings, led the way.

In September of 1991, the Department of Education cited 91st Street's history department as "astounding" and recognized the school with a citation in history. The award was only available to Blue Ribbon Schools, and only six of the 222 had been so honored. Headmistress Nancy Salisbury, Director of Academic Affairs Veronica McCaffrey, Ian Humphreys of the Upper School history department, and Sorin Feiner, an 11th grader who was extremely gifted in history, went to Washington to accept the award from President George Bush.

Students creating dishes in home economics class

Veronica McCaffrey as Head of Middle School, 1984

Beyond academics, athletics also continued to play an active role in the life of a Sacred Heart student. A compulsory physical education program was supplemented by intramural sports for the Lower and Middle Schools. The Middle and Upper Schoolers also enjoyed competitive and team sports such as basketball, gymnastics, volleyball, and track. With over 110 girls involved in competitive sports, multiple teams were required in softball, track, and basketball. Dance, paddle tennis, badminton, tag football, strength conditioning, and other sports and activities were also offered.

"Starting in fifth grade I did gymnastics five days a week on the assembly hall's 40′ by 40′ floor," says Caroline Samsen Mueller. "I also played softball and volleyball. We were serious about it, but not like today. And in those days we didn't have swimming, tennis, cross country, or hockey."

The 1980s, an excellent decade for 91st Street, culminated to some extent in July of 1988 when Saint Rose Philippine Duchesne was canonized. Five months later, on Sunday, December 4, 1988, a group of 3,000 religious, students, alumnae, their families, faculty, and staff of three Sacred Heart schools and the 42 ministries in which the religious served in the metropolitan area, gathered in St. Patrick's Cathedral for a 2:00 p.m. Mass of Thanksgiving offered by John Cardinal O'Connor.

QUALITY AND GROWTH

Over 15 years old, the Network of Sacred Heart Schools seemed to be succeeding in its goal of not only supporting the Sacred Heart schools, but of keeping alive the spirit of Sacred Heart education as the number of teaching religious continued to decline.

Nancy Salisbury's and Jane O'Connell's efforts in building fundraising to support the new curricular initiatives were aided by one of the most significant changes of Sister Salisbury's tenure: a rapidly growing student body, which nearly doubled between 1980 and 2000. "Nancy Salisbury was a tremendous educator," says Jane Maggin. "The enrollment went from 342 when she arrived to 587 when she left. But numbers are not the measure. It's the quality of education."

The growth definitely "helped the cash flow," says Jane O'Connell, "but it was a planned and concerted move. It was a commitment."

The growth was possible because Sacred Heart had developed a rapidly growing reputation under both Sister Kirby and Sister Salisbury, as could be seen in its Blue Ribbon School status and other awards and recognitions. Ninety-first Street was increasingly recognized as one of the best, and as a result, the demand became very high.

The credentials of entering students also rose with the quantity, says Jane O'Connell: "Since 1980 academic standards had become much more rigorous, at the behest of the board and administration. Now we had enough applicants to be selective. We increased the rigor, made vast improvements in science and math, added new programs. The school was becoming what people envisioned it to be."

Sister Mary Ranney echoes the sentiment. "They were wonderful years. Nancy created a whole new school. She did a wonderful job."

TOP: Alexis Brashich '86, Carolyn Carey '91, and an unidentified Lower School student
MIDDLE: Tina Vazquez '84, Coco Manoli '86, Kate Devers '86
BOTTOM: Middle School faculty member Colin Hope with students

PRIORITIES

Despite her success in bolstering the curriculum, enhancing the physical plant, and increasing the enrollment, colleagues and alumnae cite the importance of focusing not on Nancy Salisbury's accomplishments, much as they meant to Sacred Heart, but on her character and her focus on community.

"Nancy approached the challenge of leading 91st Street not by focusing upon benchmarks and statistics," wrote Stephen Sweeny, president of the College of New Rochelle, in a tribute at her retirement in 2000, "but by shoring up the concept of community within the school—encouraging better communication, identifying points where the flow between divisions required more collaboration, undertaking such simple innovations as finding space for faculty offices so that the adult community could share ideas and develop closer relationships with students."

Community was indeed one of Nancy Salisbury's highest values, and she was so gratified by the dedication in one year's yearbook to that very concept that she restated it from time to time. "We salute the school that has made community such a dynamic force in our lives," it said. "Surrounded by this gift we have felt free to develop as individuals, knowing that all the while we strove to develop our uniqueness, we were supported by the whole. The larger light engendered by a glowing community has given us each a spark with which to light our own lamps."

In the end, Nancy Salisbury never lost sight of the fact that the highest priority for a Sacred Heart school

centered upon the character, faith, and values of the girls. "We must constantly seek to balance achievement with continued striving," she wrote near the end of her tenure, "success with humility, facility with wisdom.... By being faith-centered, intellectually vibrant, socially committed, and community creating, we become self-realized, wise, and personally free."

"All of Nancy's accomplishments—in building enrollment, finance, facilities, and academics—are insignificant compared with what she as a person embodies," said Stephen Sweeny.

It was fitting that Sister Salisbury would leave as she entered, in the midst of a celebration. The 1999–2000 school year, Sister Salisbury's last, was also the year of the Society of the Sacred Heart's Bicentennial. The year-long celebration opened in October of 1999 with a Mass for the community at the Church of St. Ignatius Loyola. The next twelve months were filled with special events, congés, academic contests, and other fitting events as Sister Salisbury prepared to take her leave.

Looking around in 2000, one could see a vibrant, modern school of nearly 600 students enjoying state-of-the-art technology in a historic building, a dizzyingly broad curriculum, and extracurricular opportunities that broadened the mind and the spirit. But more importantly, it was a school that reflected the personality of its headmistress for the past two decades in "recognizing that reverence in each child, in community, in the way we function as a society," as a new member of the administration termed it in a special tribute to her at her retirement.

Some of the graduates from 1991

Students who graduated from Sacred Heart with that reverence for themselves, for others, for their society, usually achieved admission to the top colleges, like students from other private schools. But, like children of Sacred Heart before them, they also carried much more. "I realize the greatest gift Sacred Heart gave me," said Monique Cofer '97, "is a sense of myself. This is the benefit of a Sacred Heart education. This present of self-realization and self-assurance is my greatest weapon as I seek to remain empowered, effective, determined to make some difference in the world around me."

Lower School students with their lunchboxes, 1987

"Students are taught to care about each other in the nurturing environment fostered inside the school buildings. But every student also knows that she is a component of something larger. At Sacred Heart helping others is not a choice, it is an expectation that accompanies receiving such a special education."

—CAROLYN COFFEY '90

CHAPTER 7

A Living Monument

2000–2006

In the year 2000, America was a far different place than it had been in 1980 when Nancy Salisbury first took over as Headmistress. In 1980, personal computers had been less than ten years old and somewhat of a rarity in the office or school, and virtually nonexistent at home. In this pre-personal computer era, typewriters carried the load for business and for students, card catalogs listed library holdings, and the

Students in science class, 2004

vast majority of communication was by phone or U.S. mail.

By 2000, computers were ubiquitous, and work was done on various software programs. The Internet had been born and the world was wired. Card catalogs were gone, digital databases replaced file cabinets, and email largely replaced paper mail.

Several miles south of 91st Street, Wall Street, the hub of American finance, had spent the better part of a decade on a wild, uphill ride. Tech stocks and a passion for the Internet had driven the market into the stratosphere in a frenzy not unlike that of the late 1920s, and many institutions such as Sacred Heart had seen their endowments, pension funds, and other holdings rise dramatically. In 1995, Sacred Heart's endowment stood at a modest $3 million but by 2000 it had improved to $11.4 million.

Just as the revolution in technology had redefined the school, the number of religious teaching in 2000 had dwindled to just a few. Now, with Sister Salisbury's retirement, 91st Street would turn a symbolic but inevitable corner with the hiring of the first non-religious as Headmistress, Dr. Mary Blake. The Principal of the United Nations International School (UNIS) in Queens since 1991, Dr. Blake had already established a reputation as an outstanding educator, admired by colleagues as "extremely conscientious and hard-working, well grounded in independent education and possessing a global view of the world." She earned a doctorate in education from Nova Southeastern University, two master's degrees from Antioch College and the New School for Social Research, and a bachelor of science from St. John's University. In addition to her professional accomplishments, her philosophy of education and her strong moral and religious background fit well with Sacred Heart's mission and Goals and Criteria. The school had found a candidate with the necessary leadership for this period of transition and beyond.

Originally an English teacher in the public school system, Mary Blake had gone on to earn her doctorate in education and had forged a distinguished career in international studies and as an administrator at the New School and other eminent institutions. As a graduate of the Academy of St. Joseph's in Brentwood, New York, however, she felt "steeped in a similar tradition" as Sacred Heart. "There were three particular characteristics of 91st Street that helped me to know that this was the right choice. First was its spirituality, which resonated deeply with my own faith. Another important connection was the international dimension of Sacred Heart schools, with a global mission and purpose. And the third was that it was a girls' school. I was educated in a single-sex environment and believe in it. Sacred Heart was a school that combined the fundamental principles of my vision of education."

Dr. Blake assumed her new responsibilities on July 17, 2000. Speaking about her vision for education at Sacred Heart upon her arrival, Dr. Blake said, "I have come to believe that a successful academic experience informs both the body and soul. As a result, our role as educators extends beyond the classroom. The Sacred Heart students in our charge should strive to be principled, knowledgeable, inquisitive, caring, and reflective global citizens, conscious of the commonality

Dr. Mary Blake addressing alumnae at reunion

91st Street would turn a symbolic but inevitable corner with the hiring of the first non-religious as Headmistress, Dr. Mary Blake.

of their humanity, while ever mindful of their uniqueness and individuality."

Naturally, Dr. Blake was very cognizant of her role as the first non-religious headmistress and sought the best way to carry on the mission. "Recognizing that the presence of the religious is not something we can take for granted, I wanted to find ways to ensure that the tradition lives on. I gained strength and assurance from the school community, because it was clear that there was already a deep level of commitment and a real sense of ownership."

Ultimately, she believed that, from a historical perspective, the transition to another dimension of lay leadership proved to be an opportunity for faith on the part of the community. "The religious may no longer live in this magnificent building, but they live in our hearts. For the last 125 years, each generation has embraced its new role in perpetuating the mission of Sacred Heart education, and this dedication becomes a living monument to a greater good and to God."

BICENTENNIAL CELEBRATION

Like her predecessor, Sister Salisbury, Dr. Blake enjoyed the excitement of taking on the mantle of Headmistress during a great celebration. The fall of 2000 marked the Sacred Heart bicentennial, an anniversary being celebrated around the world.

The previous school year, Sister Salisbury's last, had kicked off many special bicentennial events, and the celebration continued at the start of 2000-2001, which opened with preparations for National Service Day on October 21. On this single day students, faculty, parents,

Portrait of Dr. Mary Blake, 2002

and alumnae across the Network reaffirmed their commitment to service of all kinds by dedicating their time and efforts to community service.

A month later, on November 20, representatives from three schools—91st Street, Princeton, and Greenwich—gathered for a joyful vespers service at St. Patrick's Cathedral to celebrate "200 Years of Loving." Sister Angela Bayo, who spearheaded the bicentennial celebration in the New York area, greeted over 2,300 people from the Sacred Heart community in the area, and many alumnae from other schools. "Each one of us is so much a part of that special vision that was brought to light by St. Madeleine Sophie Barat," she said. "We are that community she envisioned, a community bound by a common goal, striving always to live lives of faith, of hope, and of love."

CHALLENGES OF THE 21ST CENTURY

Dr. Blake's arrival also coincided with unprecedented growth. Because the enrollment had expanded so dramatically, the 91st Street community at the turn of the third millennium was getting ever more difficult to join. With full classes, applications were only considered for standard entry grades: pre-kindergarten, kindergarten and ninth grade. All other classes were simply closed and the increase meant that physical spaces were no longer serving the needs of the community. The refurbishing of the mansions that was done in the 1980s and 1990s, including the upgrading of communications technologies, laboratories, libraries, and other critical facilities, could not accommodate the more than 1,000 people who use the mansions every day. "We were severely overcrowded,"

Members of the Sacred Heart Habitat for Humanity chapter, 2005

says Dr. Blake, "and the clamor was getting stronger. Applications were climbing, and we wanted to offer as many girls as possible a Sacred Heart education."

Competition for those few spots was particularly difficult: only 16 percent were accepted. Barbara Root, Director of Admissions since 1987, acknowledges that the high rate of rejection sometimes feels "un-Sacred Heart" in the disappointment it causes, but adds that it is a side effect of the school's increasing desirability. "My job is first to articulate the mission of the school and what makes it special," says Root. "Sacred Heart is not for everyone, and the essence of the admissions task is to discern which families are a philosophical fit. But I get to talk about a philosophy of education that values the soul as well as the brain, wisdom as well as facility, questions as well as answers. It is this 'higher, deeper, more' aspect of Sacred Heart which most surprises, intrigues, and moves prospective parents. It is also, I think, the essential Sacred Heart difference: this process by which the Goals and Criteria shape a radical redefinition of learning, teaching, living."

Root herself has been an extraordinary ambassador for the school over the past 20 years. Many parents share the feeling of parent Jimmy Dunne, who says Root's "passion and sincerity only confirmed our opinion that 91st Street was ideal for our daughter's growth and development."

MORE SPACE: ADDING TO A LANDMARK

As a result of these growing needs the architectural firm of Murphy Burnham & Buttrick was asked to find ways to add to and modernize the existing facility without

"We are that community she envisioned, a community bound by a common goal, striving always to live lives of faith, of hope, and of love."

—ANGELA BAYO, RSCJ

Sister Ranney leads a group of RSCJ in the procession at the Bicentennial Celebration, 2001.

Campaign leaders Catherine Curry, Jack Calaman, Mary Blake, JoMarie Pica, and Vin Pica cut the ribbons to open the new spaces, 2003

> In the end, the additions provided over 10,000 square feet of new space and over 23,000 square feet of remodeled existing space.

undermining its character. The resulting changes, finished in 2003, were both dramatic and subtle. The addition of two new floors on top of the Assembly Hall allowed for the expansion of the third floor with three new classrooms and offices. Also created were a new Lower and Middle School library on the fourth floor and art classrooms for the new Fine and Performing Arts Center on the fifth floor. In addition, the basement of the Burden mansion was transformed into five science laboratories. The alleyway between the buildings, for years a catch-all space, was relocated, allowing for a new stage at the east end of the Assembly Hall. The chapel underwent renovation to allow 85 more seats, so each division of the school could worship as a unit. The Lower School art room and the photography room in the basement, no longer needed with the fifth floor studios, were combined with the old dining room to create a room seating 230—twice as many as the old dining hall. Even an exercise room was added. In the end, the additions provided over 10,000 square feet of new space and over 23,000 square feet of remodeled existing space.

"The school has come a long way from when we had one science lab for the entire school," reflects Cathy Curry '70, whose daughter now enjoys the benefits of the expanded facilities.

ANOTHER CAMPAIGN

The early cost of the additions and renovations was projected to be a staggering $25 million, an enormous cost for a school of Sacred Heart's still comparatively modest means. Clearly, another campaign was necessary, and in 1999 the silent phase of the $20 million

Campaign for Sacred Heart was begun to pay for the building expansion, augment the endowment for faculty compensation and professional development, and increase financial aid. The remainder needed would come from other sources. Parents Paul Leitner and JoMarie Pica chaired the effort, with Mimi Meehan '30 and Lucy McGrath serving as honorary co-chairs. The campaign closed on June 30, 2004, well over its goal.

A STRONG CURRICULUM

The academic program also continued to grow in depth and excellence under Dr. Blake's leadership. In the second and third year of her tenure, the school received two successful accreditation visits from the New York State Association of Independent Schools and the Sacred Heart Committee on Goals, respectively. With Dr. Blake's guidance and with board support, a scope and sequence was written, an electronic curriculum map program was incorporated, systematic curricular reviews were launched, an expansive professional development program was initiated to support faculty and staff, and an evaluation system for the adult community was implemented. Foreign language instruction now begins in kindergarten. Science and math specialists now work with the Lower School faculty, and a full music program was established in the Middle School. Seniors' college acceptances continue to reflect the caliber of the education offered at 91st Street.

Spirituality, of course, has remained central to the life of the school. "Our spiritual dimension is the continuation of the Sacred Heart mission and its expansion in the 21st century. It's simply the most vital

The Ring's the Thing

Ring Day, a long-time tradition at Sacred Heart, was celebrated by enthusiastic 11th graders last April as they prepared to enter their Senior year at 91st Street.

The traditional ring ceremony is held in the chapel, where juniors invite a special person in their lives to turn their ring—the number of turns depending on their class year—and is followed by a reception given by class parents. Sacred Heart juniors wear their ring facing inwards until graduation, at which point they symbolically turn the heart outward, thus taking the values and tenets of a Sacred Heart education out into the world.

Middle School students in the new library

component of our education," says Dr. Blake. During her tenure, the school has welcomed its first full-time chaplain, Father John Kamas, SSS, and inspired greater parental participation in the spiritual life of the school. "We are filled to capacity at the Lower School Mass. We have a beautiful early Mass on Tuesday morning. We have a spiritual book group made up of members of the adult community. We have a Wednesday prayer service where parents get together to pray for the needs of the school. The interest of our community in spiritual opportunities has never been stronger, and it gives me such a sense of joy and gratitude."

Anna Goddu '05 says spirituality is very much part of school life. "In religion classes, we studied Hebrew scriptures, the Old and New Testaments, world religions, morality, ethics, and philosophy. But even when we were very young, before we were old enough for the academic study of religion, we had children's chapel and grace before lunch. Even simply walking around the school there are religious paintings and statues, and the centrally located chapel. It all contributes to an atmosphere of faith. As a senior I went back to attend the Lower School chapel service. The little girls were singing at the top of their lungs and there was so much joy. It was completely inspiring."

ANOTHER TRANSITION

Reflecting on the last six years of the life of this school, it is clear that 91st Street has flourished. "It seems like yesterday," remarked Dr. Blake, "that we embarked on what looked then like impossible tasks: to undertake an enormously challenging construction program, mount an ambitious fundraising campaign, and maintain and improve our complex and demanding curriculum, all at the same time. Together, we accomplished a great deal in six years, and I am proud to have played a role in those achievements."

In the spring of 2006, Dr. Blake announced that she would be retiring at the end of the school year. While she was sad to depart, she did so with confidence in the future of the school. "As I prepare to leave Convent of the Sacred Heart, I feel sure that the school is well-prepared for the future and moving forward while mindful of its rich traditions and heritage."

Upon Dr. Blake's retirement, the search for a new leader for 91st Street began. Knowing that the search for a visionary leader in independent school education with outstanding academic and pedagogical credentials, as well as exceptional communication and relational skills, would take time, the Board of Trustees asked Patricia Hult, Head of Lower School and a Sacred Heart educator for nearly 30 years, to serve as Interim Head of School during the 2006–2007 school year.

In December 2006, the Board of Trustees announced the appointment of Joseph J. Ciancaglini as 91st Street's Head of School, beginning July 1, 2007. After an exhaustive process, the Search Committee felt strongly that Dr. Ciancaglini, the Head of the Sacred Heart Schools in Atherton, California, has the vision, experience, and strong understanding of the Sacred Heart mission necessary to lead 91st Street and build upon the extraordinary strengths of the school.

Paula Toner, RSCJ, former head of the Sacred Heart school in Houston, a trustee, and member of the Search

Lower School students bicycling on the newly created roofdeck

Preparation before students' First Communion, 2003

Committee, said of Dr. Ciancaglini: "In my meetings with Joe, and in speaking to those who have worked closely with him, as well as in reviewing his many accomplishments, I became convinced that Joe is an outstanding leader, that he is a person who lives the Sacred Heart mission, and that he can effectively lead 91st Street into the next chapter of its history."

As the school community prepares for a new leader and a new era in its long history, 91st Street fully embodies the spirit of Madeleine Sophie Barat and her dedication to the education of youth within a loving spiritual community. A graduate of the early 1960s or before who walks into 91st Street finds, on the surface, a far different Convent from the one she attended. Students wearing uniforms are still greeted individually by smiling teachers each morning—and the little ones still curtsy. But with over 650 girls, the arrivals process takes a little longer. The halls are no longer silent as classes pass, and there are no more prîmes. Most obviously, there are no black-robed nuns living on the third floor, silently gliding about the hallways or leading classes. And the Mistress General is now a Head of School. But that Head and the teachers have internalized the spirit of the Sacred Heart as effectively as any nun, and that spirit is passed along to the students with as much richness and care as at any time in its history.

In 2006, at its 125th anniversary, the Convent of the Sacred Heart still fully embodies the spirit of Madeleine Sophie in its dedication to the education of youth within a loving spiritual community.

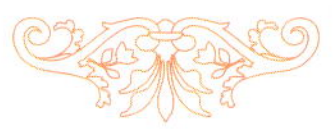

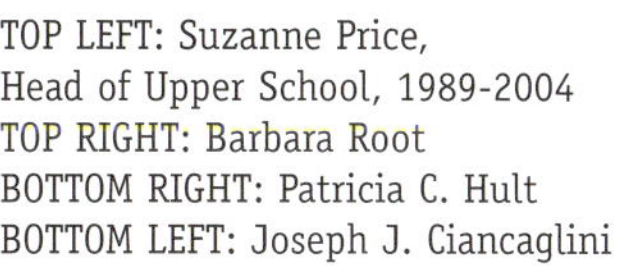

TOP LEFT: Suzanne Price,
Head of Upper School, 1989-2004
TOP RIGHT: Barbara Root
BOTTOM RIGHT: Patricia C. Hult
BOTTOM LEFT: Joseph J. Ciancaglini

EPILOGUE

An Evolving Tradition

Over 170 years ago, a reverent French nun with a heart for indigenous Americans left her beloved Alps forever. In order to carry out Madeleine Sophie Barat's at-the-time radical vision of educating young girls, Mother Rose Philippine Duchesne endured a perilous journey and subsequently a life of unimaginable hardship in the American West, where she established the Religious of the Sacred Heart in America.

TOP: First Communion at the Madison Avenue school, 1920s
MIDDLE: Hockey team of 1951
BOTTOM: Young students in reading group in the late 1960s

Because of her efforts, numerous Sacred Heart schools—free academies, free schools, Indian schools, and orphanages—were founded in the Missouri Valley and the deep South. Eventually, the strength of Mother Duchesne's vision and the power of her love ensured that her successors would continue her work, and before her death in 1852, Sacred Heart schools had been established throughout the East and into Canada. In New York City, the first academy had been established at Houston Street in 1841; others followed, including the one at Madison and 54th Street in 1881.

As schools continued to open and close over subsequent decades, the little school on Madison Avenue persevered through the turn of the century, the panic of 1907, World War I, the Roaring Twenties, and the Depression. In 1934 it moved to the Otto Kahn mansion on the corner of 91st Street and Fifth Avenue, and six years later expanded into the James Burden mansion next door at 7 East 91st.

Sixty years later, in 2006, only three religious still walk the halls of the Convent of the Sacred Heart at 91st Street. In the wake of the Second Vatican Council, Mother Barat's and Mother Duchesne's extraordinary work in educating young people—no longer always girls—lives on. Their mission is embodied in the Goals and Criteria, which serve as a guiding light for all those entrusted with fulfilling Madeleine Sophie Barat's and Philippine Duchesne's original vision.

Since the mid-1970s that leadership task at each school has fallen to administrators and boards of trustees, who are accountable to the U.S. Provincial. Because the Goals and Criteria articulate so much more

Second grade students from 1971

Where students at most schools are encouraged to compete, to rise to the top, at Sacred Heart they are encouraged to be the best they can individually be.

Parent walking with Lower School student through the entrance of building #7

profound a mission than mere academic education, the burden on these administrations and boards is unique, since it involves the spiritual, moral, and social development of young people. In one of a series of trustee reflections compiled between 2003 and 2005, one trustee wrote, "Each one of us has been asked, in effect, to be the successor to a religious order in which each member dedicated her life to God and to the whole education of children in mind, body, and spirit. They have left to us and our successors the awesome and sacred trust of continuing the mission of the Religious of the Sacred Heart."

At 91st Street, that sacred trust builds on 125 years of what Janet Erskine Stuart, RSCJ, called an "evolving tradition." From that perspective, the resultant changes over the past forty years are just a continuation of changes that have been occurring throughout the history of the order.

These changes have also sparked additional ones. For example, in the 21st century students at 91st Street are no longer defined by their neighborhoods, but spend large amounts of their time, and even more of their attention, focused on other parts of the world. And graduates, who for many years stayed predominantly within the Sacred Heart community, attending Manhattanville College, or other Catholic schools, now matriculate at a wide array of the top colleges in the country. In short, at its 125th anniversary, the oldest independent girls' school in New York City has become a school of the world, and one of the best, not only in the city but in the nation.

Of course, the quality of the education at Sacred Heart has always been a given. To understand 91st Street, or for that matter any Sacred Heart school, to understand the sacred trust, one must understand that academics are only a small part of the mission. "Here it is not just about the intellectual," says Barbara Root, "but the spiritual."

That spiritual concern is based in Saint Madeleine Sophie Barat's overwhelming focus on the individuality of each child. "A Sacred Heart educator," says Sister Judy Garson, "is someone who has internalized the guiding principles that led these schools to be what they are—with a passionate concern and love for children, a sense of the possibility of each child—the individual child." In other words, where students at most schools are encouraged to compete, to rise to the top, at Sacred Heart they are encouraged to be the best they can individually be. It is a far more personal challenge, and reaches well beyond academic achievement. "The gift of a Sacred Heart education," says Monique Cofer '97, "is a sense of myself."

Such a centered self-awareness is only the beginning, however, for much more is expected of a child of Sacred Heart. It is part of St. Madeleine Sophie Barat's mission, now embodied in the Goals and Criteria, that the personal grounding and the intellectual tools students are given over the course of their education be used to affect the world in some positive way. That is why Monique Cofer chose to enter into law and business, where she felt the skills she gained at Sacred Heart "could have the biggest impact on society."

TOP LEFT: Nun assisting a child with her meal
TOP RIGHT: Sister Moon from the Madison Avenue School
BOTTOM LEFT: Sister Joan Kirby celebrating Sacred Heart centennial with students
BOTTOM RIGHT: A group of nuns traveling, 1950s

Pre-kindergarten students playing on the new roof deck

In 2003, Phil Gelston, a trustee, offered a prayer concerning this profound, multitiered mission. "When, with your guidance, we succeed in our mission of implementing the Goals and Criteria, our students, as a group, will contribute to the creation of a world with less of the fear, fanaticism, intolerance, injustice, and suffering so dominant today. And maybe, possibly, one single child in these halls may grow up to provide the individual leadership that truly changes our nation and our world."

That prayer is being answered. Despite the many changes, over 200 years after Saint Madeleine Sophie Barat first articulated her vision and nearly 190 years after Saint Philippine Duchesne brought it to America, the Convent of the Sacred Heart at 91st Street in New York continues to foster a reverence for the individuality of every single child, a limitless reservoir for hope, and the unbounded capacity for having a positive impact on the world.

"When I was at 91st Street, I was given a powerful message: There's no reason to believe that women are not as empowered to achieve success, whether that success is in the family, or a career, or the volunteer community."

—EMILY RAFFERTY '67

Graduates from the Class of 2001 preparing for their traditional class photo

Goals and Criteria

for the Sacred Heart Schools
in the United States

GOAL I

Schools of the Sacred Heart commit themselves to educate to a personal and active faith in God.

1. Rooted in the love of Jesus Christ, the school promotes a personal relationship with God and fosters the spiritual lives of its members.
2. The school seeks to form its students in the attitudes of the heart of Jesus expressed in respect, compassion, forgiveness and generosity.
3. The entire school program explores one's relationship to God, to self, to others, and to all creation.
4. Opening themselves to the transforming power of the Spirit of God, members of the school community engage in personal and communal prayer, reflection and action.
5. The entire school program affirms that there is meaning and value in life and fosters a sense of hope in the individual and in the school community.
6. The school fosters inter-religious acceptance and dialogue by educating to an understanding of and deep respect for the religions of the world.
7. The school presents itself to the wider community as a Christ-centered institution and as an expression of the mission of the Society of the Sacred Heart.

GOAL II

Schools of the Sacred Heart commit themselves to educate to a deep respect for intellectual values.

1. The school develops and implements a curriculum based on the Goals and Criteria, educational research and ongoing evaluation.
2. The school provides a rigorous education that incorporates all forms of critical thinking and inspires a life-long love of learning.
3. The school program develops aesthetic values and the creative use of the imagination.
4. The faculty utilizes a variety of teaching and learning strategies that recognizes the individual needs of the students.
5. The school provides ongoing professional development for faculty and staff.
6. Members of the school community model and teach ethical and respectful use of technology.

GOAL III

Schools of the Sacred Heart commit themselves to educate to a social awareness which impels to action.

1. The school educates to a critical consciousness that leads its total community to analyze and reflect on the values of society and to act for justice.
2. The school offers all its members opportunities for direct service and advocacy and instills a life-long commitment to service.
3. The school is linked in a reciprocal manner with ministries among people who are poor, marginalized and suffering from injustice.
4. In our multicultural world, the school prepares and inspires students to be active, informed, and responsible citizens locally, nationally, and globally.
5. The school teaches respect for creation and prepares students to be stewards of the earth's resources.

GOAL IV

Schools of the Sacred Heart commit themselves to educate to the building of community as a Christian value.

1. The school implements an ongoing plan for educating both adults and students in the heritage and mission of Sacred Heart education.
2. The school promotes a safe and welcoming environment in which each person is valued, cared for and respected.
3. Adult members of the school model and teach skills needed to build community and practice clear, direct and open communication.
4. The school has programs that teach the principles of nonviolence, conflict resolution and peacemaking.
5. The school makes a deliberate effort to recruit students and employ faculty and staff of diverse races, ethnicities and backgrounds.
6. The financial aid program effectively supports socioeconomic diversity.
7. The school participates actively in the national and international networks of Sacred Heart schools.

GOAL V

Schools of the Sacred Heart commit themselves to educate to personal growth in an atmosphere of wise freedom.

1. All members of the school community show respect, acceptance and concern for themselves and for others.
2. School policies and practices promote self-discipline, responsible decision making, and accountability.
3. Students grow in self-knowledge and develop self-confidence as they learn to deal realistically with their gifts and limitations.
4. School programs provide for recognizing, nurturing and exercising leadership in its many forms.
5. The school provides opportunities for all members of the community to share their knowledge and gifts with others.
6. All members of the school community take personal responsibility for balance in their lives and for their health and well-being.

APPENDIX

SUPERIORS

Sarah Jones, *1881–1885*
Margaret Hoey, *1886–1890, 1892–1895, 1901–1902*
Fannie Elder, *1891*
Sarah Randall, *1896–1900*
Martha Raleigh, *1903*
Addie Smith, *1904–1908*
Frances Molloy, *1909–1916*
Katherine Finnegan, *1917–1922*
Gabrielle de Roquefeuille, *1923–1928*
Berthe Padberg, *1929–1931*
Jean Levis, *1932–1933, 1940–1945*
Ellen Green, *1934–1939*
Eleanor Mulqueen, *1946–1952*
Margaret Shea, *1953–1958, 1963–1967*
Marie Louise Schroen, *1959–1962*
Mary Ranney, *1968*
Eileen McDonnell, *1969–1973*

MISTRESS GENERALS

Fannie Edler, *1881, 1891*
Marie Ange Bondroit, *1882–1886*
Louise Bouvier, *1887–1889*
Marie Valorge, *1890*
Irene Robinson, *1892*
Kathleen Harris, *1893–1895*
Darah Randall, *1896–1900*
Elizabeth Atkinson, *1901–1902*
Martha Raleigh, *1903*
Nora Farley, *1904–1906*
Jeanne de Traverse, *1907–1922*
Edith Coman, *1923–1928*
Berthe Padberg, *1929*
Sarah Egert, *1930–1931*
Elizabeth White, *1932–1935*
Mary McCarthy, *1936–1938*
Margaret Shea, *1939–1942*
Jane Saul, *1943–1950*
Cora Brady, *1951–1953*
Beatrice Brennan, *1954–1958*
Ursula McAghon, *1959–1961*
Maraget Brown, *1962–1968*
Mary Ellen Harmon, *1968–1969*
Joan Kirby, *1969–1973*

HEADMISTRESSES

Joan Kirby, *1974–1980*
Nancy Salisbury, *1981–2000*
Mary Blake, *2000–2006*

HEAD OF SCHOOL

Patricia C. Hult, *2006–2007*
Joseph J. Ciancaglini, *2007–*

CHAIRS OF THE BOARD OF TRUSTEES

John M. Felleman, *1976–1979*
Alfred Y. Morgan III, *1979–1982*
Winthrop Rutherfurd, Jr., *1982–1986*
Richard Winfield, *1987–1990*
Terrence Schwab, *1990–1993*
Emily K. Rafferty, *1993–1997*
Mary Anne Boyd, *1997–2000*
Hilary Adams, *2001–2002*
Kenneth F. Cooper, *2002–2003*
Vincent T. Pica II, *2003–2005*
Laurette Bryan, *2004–2005*
Cornelia Thornburgh, *2005–*

Several publications were used in researching the history of Convent of the Sacred Heart, including:

Changing Habits, by V.V. Harrison
Convent of the Sacred Heart, New York City: 1881–1981, A History
Education of Catholic Girls, by Janet Erskine Stuart
Growing Good Catholic Girls, by Christine Trimingham Jack
Madeleine Sophie Barat: A Life, by Phil Kilroy
The Many Lives of Otto Kahn, by Mary Jane Matz
Philippine Duchesne: Frontier Missionary of the Sacred Heart, by Louise Callan
Saint Madeleine Sophie Barat, by C.E. Maguire

PHOTOGRAPHY CREDITS

Every effort has been made to give proper credit for each of the photographs in this book. We regret that many which came from school archives are unmarked and therefore not attributable.

David Heald • David Heald Photographs, Redding Ridge, CT
Cover: Front and Back; Pgs. 7, 128-129, 132-133, 154.

Johnathan M. Linton • Johnathan M. Linton Fine Art, Chatham, NJ
Dust Jacket Cover: Bottom Right.

John Montana • John Montana Photography, New York, NY
Dust Jacket Cover: Bottom Left, Back Cover; Pgs. 1, 2, 8, 10-11, 20-21, 64, 80-81, 114-115, 122.

Juliana Thomas • Juliana Thomas Photography, New York, NY
Dust Jacket Cover: Upper Left, Upper Right, Center; Pgs. 5, 61, 67, 71, 134, 135, 136-137, 138, 140, 141, 142, 143, 144, 145, 146-147, 150, 152, 153, 160.

Janet Traynor • *Pg. 116*

LITTLE MANUAL
in Honor of
ST. MADELEINE
SOPHIE BARAT
NOVENA
OF
CONFIDENCE
LORD Jesus! Through the intercession of St. Madeleine Sophie, to Your Sacred Heart I confide . . . (this intention). Only look. . . . Then do what Your Heart inspires. . . . Let Your Heart decide. . . . I count on it. . . . I trust in it. . . . I throw myself on its mercy. . . . Lord Jesus! You will not fail me.
St. Madeleine Sophie, by your tender love for Jesus and your sympathy for all in trouble, obtain for us the favors we implore, especially the grace to increase daily in very fervent love of the Sacred Heart of Jesus.
St. Madeleine Sophie
in her later years.
ST. MADELEINE
SOPHIE BARAT
Feast — May 25
ST. MADELEINE Sophie Barat, whose parents were simple French peasants, was born in 1779, and, after a life devoted to the service of her Lord, died in 1865. Because of her saintly life and works she was canonized by Pope Pius XI in 1925.
From her childhood St. Madeleine Sophie had a tender love for the Divine Heart of Jesus, which was to crystallize in the foundation of the Society of the Sacred Heart in 1800. She governed the Society as Superior General for over sixty years, unceasingly urging her Religious to have an insatiable desire to give themselves to the utmost for the glory of the Sacred Heart.
St. Madeleine Sophie willingly bore many grievous crosses, misunderstandings from without and within, humiliations, sickness, difficulties and opposition — eager to suffer for love of the Sacred Heart.
St. Madeleine Sophie practiced humility and charity to a heroic degree. Remarkable for her gracious kindness to all while on earth, she continues to obtain both spiritual and temporal blessings from the Sacred Heart for those who invoke her aid.

THOUGHTS and SAYINGS

of

St. Madeleine Sophie Barat

Pride displeases our Lord more than anything else. Why? Because the devil is our Lord's enemy, and the devil is pride itself.

There is room for all in that wide wound in the Heart of Jesus, but its secret depths are for the little and lowly ones.

There is no virtue without humility, the characteristic virtue of the Heart of Jesus.

We find our way into the Heart of Jesus by calming our passions and by becoming humble.

Humility is the best preparation for Holy Communion.

God takes His delight in a heart that has grown deep by humility and wide by charity.

Humility is the special virtue of great souls, and it will supply all that is wanting to those who are not great.

To humble ourselves is the best way to put things right, even with those whom we have in no way wronged.

If we succeeded, once for all, in becoming humble and self-forgetful, all would be well.

When God asks a sample, give Him the whole piece.

Every delay with God is a kind of refusal.

The graces and consolations which God grants to His elect are not written in the Book of Life, but their battles and victories are there.

When we have lost neither Heaven nor hope, what else matters?

It is not easy to satisfy everybody; let us do our best, and remain at peace.

We are blind in matters that concern ourselves; let us often say to our Lord: "Lord, that I may see."

Let us cast our care on our Lord, and ask Him to act for us; then everything will come right; that which we do of ourselves is full of defects.

God does not reward success, over which we have no control; He looks to our intention.

To consecrate one's heart to Jesus is to consecrate it to happiness.

Nothing effaces sin like love.

Prayer is the shield of the soldier of Jesus Christ.

Let us pray and sanctify ourselves; it is for this that we are on earth.

Prayer and patience are the two means that Jesus gives us to triumph over all obstacles.

If we seek God alone, the rest will cause us neither joy nor sorrow.

Prayer without sacrifice is worth little or nothing.

Let us seek God's glory at all costs. What are our sacrifices compared to those our Lord made in order to save us.

Prayer is the shield of the soldier of Jesus Christ, it is an invincible defence.

The soul's true happiness is found in self-sacrifice for the glory of God.

It should be our ambition in life to glorify the Heart of Jesus.

Do not bargain with our Lord; give all and you will receive all. And what is our poor little all, beside that great all, the Heart of our Lord?

Everything is good, if it gives glory to our Lord.

Ask our Lord constantly to make Himself King in your heart, and by your means in the hearts of others. These two thoughts must not be separated. The essential is that He should reign, and that by your means.

Strive every moment to do something more and better for the glory of the Sacred Heart.

The times in which we live call for fervor, fidelity and generosity. Let us begin, for if we do not attain this threefold aim, all will be lost time and trouble.

I can do all in Him who strengtheneth me; strong with the strength of the Heart of Jesus, what can I fear? Hell itself has no power to harm me.

To please creatures is the mere shadow of happiness; true happiness lies in pleasing God.

Look upon that day as wasted in which you have suffered nothing for Jesus.

The heart's best security is trust in God alone.

A single soul saved is worth more than our life.

When we seek God, we already possess what we seek.

Saints are less admirable for the holiness of their lives than for the courage with which they rise after each fall.

If you seek God alone constantly, you will find Him easily.

Sancta Magdelena Sophie
(Statue in St. Peter's, Rome.)